the SIX QUESTIONS

That You Better Get Right
The Answers are the Keys to Your Success

JULIE EDMONDS & MICHELL SMITH

New York

the SIX QUESTIONS

That You Better Get Right The Answers are the Keys to Your Success

ISBN 978-1-61448-223-9 paperback
ISBN 978-1-61448-224-6 eBook
Library of Congress Control Number: 2012932264

Morgan James Publishing
The Entrepreneurial Publisher
5 Penn Plaza, 23rd Floor,
New York City, New York 10001
(212) 655-5470 office • (516) 908-4496 fax
www.MorganJamesPublishing.com

Cover photo by
Camellia Teague
www.fortworthphotography.com

Illustrations by
Danie-J
www.danie-j.com

Cover Design by:
Rachel Lopez
www.r2cdesign.com

Interior Design by:
Bonnie Bushman
bonnie@caboodlegraphics.com

TABLE OF CONTENTS

Foreword

by Jay Conrad Levinson

When I make a presentation on "Guerrilla Marketing," I almost always close it with a question and answer session.

But it's a different kind of session: I ask the questions and I give the answers.

The reason I've structured it like that is that there are some critical questions that must be answered, and if the audience doesn't ask them and I don't ask them, they may never know the answers. So I ask the questions.

That's just what Julie Edmonds and Michell Smith have done is this remarkable book. Simply reading it will make you a more remarkable person.

Benjamin Franklin was one of the profound thinkers who said that the three hardest things in life are steel, diamonds and knowing yourself. This book can't do much about those first two hard things, but it can do a whole lot about the third one.

In truth, it's you who will do the heavy lifting with that one. But you can do that heavy lifting with one hand tied behind your back. All that's required is that you ask a question and then answer it as good as you can.

There are no wrong answers. If you answer the question, that's the right answer – because we suspect you're too bright to fool yourself. We believe that because here you are, voluntarily, at the edge of an abyss that has no bottom. It's no place for pretenders.

Everyone knows that.

I, personally, love the population of the planet. Hardly anybody is doing the wrong thing intentionally. But that same hardly anybody isn't really sure that they're doing the right thing.

Thank Julie and Michell for putting an end to that sad reality. As a team, they're going to put the right questions in front of you. As the key member of that team, you're going to put the right answers up in your brain.

Once you've done that, you'll have taken the first baby steps in the direction of true success in life.

It sounds good, but it gets better. As they say in the world of marketing, but wait, there's more!

You'll have started out in the right direction by asking only the first question. Five more await you on your journey—five more simple but nuclear powered questions—each with its own answer that you—and only you have.

Once you've completed the book and answered the questions, you'll have the self-knowledge that Benjamin Franklin says is so hard to acquire.

He would have been proud of you—but not as proud as you'll be of yourself.

Jay Conrad Levinson

DeBary, Florida 2012

Introduction

As a woman in a man's world, learning to navigate the realm of business and leadership was comparable to charting a course to a yet undiscovered planet in another solar system. Starting out as young entrepreneurs, business success was something we both yearned for, however, knowing what to do and figuring out what route to take was a guessing game. It was a guessing game until we discovered *the Six Questions.*

Now before we even get to *the Six Questions,* we have some very important issues to address particularly with women that we sometimes sabotage ourselves with. The odds are that we put ourselves last. The odds are that we believe being a woman will make it harder for us to succeed. The odds are that we feel guilty and consider it selfish to take care of ourselves at times. The odds are that we feel we need someone else to make us feel loved. The odds are that we feel unappreciated by some people in our lives and we allow this to deflate us … We need to make the odds even, before we can properly begin.

The Six Questions starts by asking us what we want. As women, we want it all, and too often feel the need to apologize or feel guilty for that. That way of thinking has kept us caged, in our minds and in our lives, somehow feeling undeserving of putting what we want on our priority list. We need to address how wrong this is before we go anywhere … and celebrate the beauty and the power of the X Factor. The capacity that we have as emotional creatures is a magnificence of the highest kind. Knowing this is required before we ask ourselves *the Six Questions*. Believing this to be true is necessary before we can find the right answers.

Each of *the Six Questions* must be asked and answered honestly from the heart before you move onto the next one. If you do not like the answer, learn to change it. Getting the right answers to these questions is required and it must feel right; getting them wrong carries too high of a price. You will get an entirely different set of answers to these questions if you are asking from your head rather than your heart.

Question Number One: How clear are you on what you want? Knowing the answer to this question with complete clarity is the most important first step in designing or redesigning your life. Answering this question alone takes commitment—commitment to learn the truth. Defining a result that you are truly passionate about is one of the biggest gifts you can give yourself.

Question Number Two: How committed are you to getting it? This question is a heavy one. If you are really serious about what you want, ninety nine percent commitment is not enough. Connecting and feeling a resolute, unwavering conviction to what you want is the only way you have a chance at creating it -your commitment level is where you have influence over that chance. Commitment must exist when the chips are down, when you lose focus on your goals, and when the obstacles are almost too much to bear. Commitment is how you begin to win… This is your life we are talking about.

Question Number Three: How do you see yourself? The truth in the answer to this question is powerful too. How we see ourselves affects every single thing in our worlds. We need to love what we see. Perhaps this may take work ... but—if we don't do it, who will? It's time to see yourself as the person who is capable of living the life you dream about. To accomplish the goals you have set, you need to see yourself as the person who can.

Question Number Four: How are you managing your surroundings? Relationships, circumstances, obstacles, and successes are not accidental. This question asks you about the people you are surrounded by, the choices you make, the perspective you have, and your outlook in your life. Do you like what you have in your life? Do you remove what you don't like? How tolerant are you? Opportunity is everywhere dependent on your perspective.

Question Number Five: How well do you handle things when you feel you aren't winning? Life is filled with setbacks, tough people, losses, and unexpected mishaps. Sometimes we get lost, sometimes we get angry, and sometimes we misinterpret what is happening. How you manage your emotions and the things in your life during tough times dictates your path to a huge degree. Your ability to manage these determines your chances of success.

Question Number Six: Would you bet on yourself to win? The honesty of this answer is inescapable. Acquiring skills, strengthening your mindset and learning to have a perspective that will serve you can be easy. But make no apologies for whom you are; bet on yourself to win.

The grass can be the greenest right under your own two feet... this is the truth for everyone.

Now, as women, we understand and are empathetic to other women's feelings. We feel, we analyze, we emote, we hint without expressing what we really feel, we dismiss, we say we are fine, we overanalyze and we over-explain sometimes to hide from ourselves, let alone everyone else. Then we get jobs, husbands, kids, friends, more ways to accomplish things, more people to take care of, and more people to feel empathic to. Now with all these people, relationships and strategies, it is no wonder how easy it is for us to get lost inside the hearts and minds of others and deny our own wants and needs.

Throughout our lives, we've already proven that we know how to ask questions—lots of questions. Asking the *right* questions is the first step to designing our own lives. More importantly, however, finding the *right answers* is how we create a path to personal freedom.

MAKING THE ODDS EVEN…

(This part's for the girls)
How the battle is won …

Chapter 1:
We Want it All

Chapter 2:
The X Factor

Chapter 1

We Want it All

Michell

We do want it all. The feelings we crave … when our hearts feel that they could beat straight out of our chests, and that deep connectedness that we long for in all of the things in our lives: the passion of love, the warmth of friendship, the fulfillment of contribution and the joy of accomplishment; the seduction of attraction and the thrill of excitement. We want to feel them all.

We perform thousands of tasks, one following another, in a harmonious pursuit of these basic emotions that we so crave in the honest depths of ourselves. We want it all. We want it all so much it can be intoxicating … We are smart, loving, generous, kind, forgiving, ambitious, industrious, creative and compassionate women, and we can be overwhelmed by what we long for in our lives. Sometimes we can even judge ourselves so harshly it hurts … sometimes.

Isn't it interesting the way we work? The way we think and feel and choose things for ourselves? Isn't it amazing how right we are all the time and yet, sometimes, how wrong we can get things? Being the exclusive architects of our lives, choosing every detail, and at times killing ourselves working hard in the pursuit of the things we want … we think.

I compare navigating through my twenties with the first time I tried playing dual- analogue video games on the new x-box. I spent most of my time running in circles, out of control, looking straight up trying to regain my bearings while getting shot at by adversaries that I couldn't even see. I was looking for love and belonging, passion and purpose, and I bent myself in any way I thought would bring those things into my life. The "what" didn't matter much, the "why" didn't exist yet, the "who" was almost as irrelevant … the only thing that mattered was how I felt, and how I longed to feel.

Retrospectively I admire the theatrics of a young life purely driven by emotional power, because of the honesty and clarity of it.

Our Challenge

The challenge is that as women we have a high desire for feeling fulfilled. We map our lives by how we feel and how we want to feel. When we turn off emotionally we begin to make decisions outside ourselves, living on autopilot on a safe, pre-selected route until we can handle driving again. Some of us don't go through this as dramatically, but for others … we get really good at believing that we are just … fine.

The truth still remains; we do want it all, and I am not talking about material things, positions or titles but the real truth that lies in every one of us—to feel loved and important, successful and sexy, attractive and appreciated, treasured, protected, safe … and still free. The realization that perhaps some of us dove into a career, fulfilling most of these needs by realizing corporate success because it was a safer place to pursue them after a damaging breakup, is an interesting thought to ruminate on … Each of us will find these feelings in the pursuit of different things, but our finding them is the key to feeling them.

Odds are we don't spend enough time even thinking about this. Odds are, we spend more time thinking about what everybody else in our lives wants and needs, and we use our ability to help them get it as the gauge to determine our own value.

Some of us are so busy being busy, that we might have gotten lost somewhere along the way. What we want gets pushed around by what we "have to do." We can be good at filling ourselves and our lives by taking care of others and leaving ourselves as an afterthought. It's even what some of us believe that we should do—as a sense of duty to the other people in our lives. Or perhaps it is to instead avoid answering for ourselves what we really think of where we are.

That's just plain wrong.

Perhaps we all know that … if we are prepared to be honest with ourselves.

Some of us feel guilty even thinking about what we really want, as though it is in some way too selfish or un-nurturing of us. It is as though we were trained from the time we were little girls—when we played with dolls and took care of our animals—that we were meant to be caregivers for others exclusively, as part of our nature. This is indeed a beautiful part of our nature but it is absolutely not at the sacrifice of our own needs for fulfillment. From the time we were little, we learned how easy it was to get love by being helpful, and so began the lifelong currency trade of affection—a trade that some of us lost ourselves in. There is no point in being upset if this is in part true for any of us; just consider that it is interesting to learn a new way to trade currency, and to discover in the process that investing in ourselves yields the highest of all returns … especially when the "economy" is unstable.

The danger in counting on other people to feed our own happiness is like expecting another country to finance our country. That doesn't seem to work well anywhere….

Odds are, we will slip off of our priority list multiple times throughout our lives. There are a thousand reasons for this: new job, new relationship, demanding career, family needs, friends in need; you name it—we give in to it. We are very helpful. A new problem or goal arises and we dive in—completely. And just like when we dive into water—we can completely disappear. We need to remember to check in with ourselves, and get back to the surface … for ourselves. It's not that everyone else doesn't count; it's just that we count too.

Both of us have been there. In fact both of us have been a lot of places. We have earned our PHDs in *Refusing to back down … Refusing to give up … and Refusing to compromise ourselves* in the process—a triple major if you will. In our early twenties, we wanted to take on the world. We wanted it all. We wanted finances, fitness, fun, and freedom. We also wanted fairness in business with our male counterparts and we were ready to play with the big dogs. We wanted to win and we were prepared to fight. We had a purpose but had no idea how to get there.

Tired of waitressing and tending bar, we both individually started jobs in outside, door-to- door, commission-only sales, selling products for hospitality and telecom clients. There was no glamour in it to start. Most of our friends and family thought we were crazy, but we were entrepreneurs and what is life if you can't take risks? We both were trained by amazing teams of people and learned about communication, the power of honesty in dialogue, how to accomplish goals and being rewarded for results instead of time spent. Our lives completely changed, and our ambitions grew … the fact that we didn't understand how to "operate" our emotionally driven selves yet made for a further complicated climb through the corporate benchmarks.

The teams of people we each trained were like rock stars and soon after starting our door-to-door jobs, we both signed contracts with the same supplier and opened our own businesses. This is how we met each other. Our suppliers provided us with clients, and our teams went out to "the field" and sold the services.

For the next decade, we fought. We grew, we struggled, we succeeded and we failed. We built and we lost. We learned the most about ourselves though, and how we felt through it all. Having a wing woman to talk to about EVERYTHING made us realize how often we were discussing how we felt. We learned to use this as a baseline for our progress. How did we feel? How did we want to feel? What could we do to ensure this shift in feeling occurred?

Interesting.

And what did that do to EVERYTHING else in our lives? Even more interesting …

Learning to become experts at being successful and happy women became the primary focus of pursuit. Somewhere along the way what we individually wanted got swallowed up by what everyone around us wanted. Working incessantly to satisfy goals of members of our teams took priority over our individual goals. Feeling selfish even considering that we needed time for ourselves was a routine ritual, and not taking the time for ourselves was our routine mistake.

We learned that almost every time we felt off track it was as a result of somehow removing ourselves from our priority list. The odds are better that we will feel more fulfilled when we keep ourselves at the top of our priority list.

We pursued career success, but were constantly aware that our goals changed as our feelings changed, our hearts yearned for something that our careers alone could not provide. Paying attention allowed us to recognize this. Understanding how we "work" permitted us to go after it.

Making the odds even begins with giving ourselves permission to want things, for ourselves, alone—guilt free. Embracing the concept that this is required, that we deserve to be cared for this way, is freeing.

We want it all and that's okay—so how do we begin to get it?

Chapter 2

THE X FACTOR

Michell

The *X factor* is the answer.

We are so fortunate to have it; our intuition, our emotional awareness, our perceptive natures all supported by an internal strength of an almost supernatural degree.

"Y" is being a woman so different than being a man?

Thank the extra chromosome. They got the Y. We got the X. X has always marked the spot where the treasure lies—where the answer is. This time it does too.

Being a woman is a beautiful thing. Being a creature that is ruled by emotion is a beautiful thing. It's our own responsibility though, to learn how to navigate and master this most magnificent, feeling creature so that we may experience the love and lives we so desire.

Designing our lives to withstand the challenges we face, survive the losses and sadnesses, setbacks and painful times can all be done by ensuring that we choose to build a life that provides us with a stronger base of fulfilling experiences and rewards. It is a life which delivers love, joy, happiness, accomplishment, contribution, value, honor, pride and connection. The world inside of us is more heavily weighted on the side of fulfillment, allowing us to spend the most time feeling wonderful. *That is our number one job as a woman.*

Looking for these things outside of ourselves is our biggest mistake. Feelings that arrive when others project them on us are just short term forces of nature. The feelings that we generate inside of ourselves are the only ones that have a constant presence. If we truly feel good about ourselves, these feelings are present even when we are alone, away from the influence of those around us.

The X Factor—Immeasurable self love. The love we have available for others is limitless. The depth of the love that we have for a child is indescribably, consumingly, painfully, overwhelmingly all encompassing … an actual physical presence of power. The love we have available for ourselves is this exact same love. Our capacity is endless.

We attain the power of the X Factor only when we learn to allow this love also to grow *for ourselves*. This is when we become not an object of love, but a manufacturing plant of lovingness for our own lives and the fortunate ones that we fill our lives with.

We must accept the fact that X creatures and Y creatures process and operate very differently. X creatures are run by emotion. We feel, consider, contemplate, notice, analyze continuously and draw conclusions that are unique. But we can get upset with others for what we IMAGINE they are thinking. Why? We process everything through our current emotional state—like a computer antivirus program. This is dangerous if we're not feeling good. It is even more dangerous if we ACTIVELY LOOK to prove that others are up to no good—we will find whatever we look for. It is most dangerous when we damage relationships by accusing and persecuting others based on our imaginings alone.

X creatures often focus on others, equating everything emotionally, and dissecting the tiniest of transactions to an exhausting degree. This can cause trouble for us Xs, if we depend on others first to give us the love and approval that we crave in our lives. When they don't, we are consumed by the reasons behind why … and this journey only descends into places of "less," never to places of "more." Most of the time, the only way we will receive all of the love in our lives that we crave, is if we provide most of it for ourselves in the first place.

Y creatures process based on logic. If there is no logical equation requiring analysis at the moment, there is no processing going on. Really. No antivirus software either. Seriously.

This is partly why Y creatures think that we are crazy … where they think, we feel … we always feel, and want to talk about it to explore those feelings. When we want to change how we feel, we want to express how we feel first. In most cases, this is what girlfriends are for!

We have different operating systems. We are hard wired that way—which in a lot of cases means it is not our fault! There is so much miscommunication that occurs between species it is kind of like asking a Mac to be compatible with a PC … or an Xbox to be compatible with a Play station…. Men are direct and women are indirect in the way they communicate. Learning this and accepting it is a key in interpreting each other. Successfully interpreting each other is required for success in any relationship or on any playing field.

In business, choosing to play ball with the big boys, as a woman, brings with it a certain risk. You have to feel genuinely confident about who you are already and the abilities you have; learning to navigate the corporate battlefield as a woman is no easy task, and it's nobody else's responsibility to make it easier for you.

We made so many changes as we grew up through our careers in order to see ourselves as strong business people. We wore pantsuits and ponytails, dark colors and high collared shirts, carried big briefcases and left the perfume at home....

It didn't much matter. That's when we realized that no one else determines our ability to succeed—we do. How we honestly feel about ourselves is the biggest driver of our results. Add that to commitment and performance, and then we actually have a shot at being a player. So, we don't dress in grey in order to blend in and not be seen as women any more.... If they're going to imagine us naked, they're going to do it anyways.

Performance and ability to drive revenue and deliver is how you get noticed. Demonstrating character and remaining professional while under pressure gets you respect. Keeping your word and delivering on promises builds trust. Taking risks and demonstrating loyalty commands a following.

The size of your network of influence gives you leverage. These realities do not care if you are male or female; they are simple truths to the world of business.

The X Factor is our advantage, when we learn to understand how to control it. Our willingness to be emotionally aware can be our most powerful asset. Learning to harness the power of the X factor is a life-changing venture.

Making the odds even means truly embracing our assets as wonderful, capable women. We are not the weaker sex, not emotionally or intuitively, not from a mental strength perspective or a capability perspective. We must stop permitting any thinking that being female somehow prevents us. It's our own thinking this that creates this as a reality.

The X Factor is where the magic lies.

The X Factor is how we get it all.

Harnessing the power of the X Factor is how the battle is won.

The Six Questions are waiting …

THE SIX QUESTIONS

Each of these questions must be asked and answered honestly, before you move on to the next one. If you do not like an answer, learn to change it. Getting the right answers to these questions is required; getting them wrong carries too high a price.

But before you get started, quickly come visit us for a warm welcome from Julie and Michell. Scan the code or visit the link @ www.julieandmichell.com/launch_welcome.html

Question Number One:

HOW CLEAR ARE YOU ON WHAT YOU WANT?

Knowing the answer to this question with complete clarity is like enabling the missile lock on a high-powered weapon of overwhelming capability.

Chapter 3

GETTING CLARITY

Julie

Question number one is:
"How clear are you on what you want?"

Have you ever felt lost in the middle, bored or depressed from the same old routine? Are you overwhelmed, stressed, and confused at what direction you want or scared of your future? Do you feel as though something is missing in your life or are you going in a million different directions? A big part of the answer to why you are feeling this way is lack of direction.

Getting clarity is the first step in designing or redesigning our life. Getting clarity is the most important first step, and we have to be willing to take time and give ourselves direction. It's actually pretty easy. Our excuses for not getting clarity include being way too busy, pretending to act like we know what we want already, or skating around the idea of what's important to us. It's easy to stay really busy so that we don't have to stop and think or feel. All of this is too big of an excuse to ignore our own callings.

You can have everything you want in life. It just requires the right approach and a healthy dose of confidence. And, equally important is to first realize that what you want should always serve you in the most positive, healthy way.

There are five steps in getting clarity.

STEP 1 on Getting Clear: ***Slow down and clear your mind.*** Take deep breaths, and take some quiet time for yourself every day. This will help you clear your head and let your heart speak to you. When our minds are free from the clutter, it's easy to hear our heart speak.

It's easy to put yourself last on the list and to continue our same, mundane daily routines because it's comfortable, familiar and without risk, or it simply pays the bills. Fantasizing about another life, telling ourselves that "one day ..." or thinking that others are just lucky or more fortunate than us, is our own justification to escape making a change. There is beauty and serendipity in life not knowing everything we want and allowing room for life's big surprise gifts; however, direction, vision and clarity open those doors to change.

This is an important lesson in learning to find clarity. Sometimes we are so extraordinarily busy accomplishing everything on our task list, running ourselves ragged, and taking care of everyone else around us that there is no energy left to concentrate on ourselves. At this point, it's painful to even just think. There were many mornings I recall waking up exhausted from just being so extraordinarily busy trying to escape my own self. I had raccoon eyes from my makeup, one shoe on the floor, the other one lost in the abyss, and I was still wearing my business suit. My cell phone and laptop were on the bed next to me—batteries dead of course.

The Chocolate Chip Cookie Syndrome

STEP 2 on Getting Clear: ***Define the "why's" behind what you are seeking.*** You want to make sure that the things in life you are asking for are the right things for you.

When I was a kid, if my mother asked me what I wanted for dinner, my answer every time was "chocolate chip cookies!" I also wanted to be Wonder Woman and fly in an invisible jet. How did I know that that wasn't the right thing for me at that age or that I was being unrealistic? All I knew was that chocolate chip cookies smelled and tasted delicious! How could that possibly be the wrong thing for me?

As an adult, I realized that I was asking for those metaphoric chocolate chip cookies when I was asked what I wanted in life. How do I know what isn't good for me? How does anyone? Asking for something just because it's a quick escape from your current lifestyle or issues is the surest way to end up back in the same place you started or even backwards. It's easy to start a new relationship than work on an existing one. We want to ask for things that aid us in moving forward and guiding an evolution from within.

Those same metaphoric cookies show up everywhere in our lives, from seeking relationships and choosing career paths, to spending and buying items we may not need, to going places or making decisions, all without thinking of the consequences. How clear are you on what you want?

Understanding how to be clear on what's right for us is part of designing and redesigning our lives. One of the easiest ways to figure out what's right for you is to figure out the "why's" behind what you are seeking.

- Why do I want to run my own business?
- Why do I want to look good?
- Why do I want a particular man in my life?
- Why do I want a certain position with my career?

After identifying the "whys" behind what I was seeking, I realized that finding fulfillment was from the inside out—but all that time I was looking from the outside in. I was taking the wrong approach.

We always want to choose what we think feels good in the moment. We are driven by impulse factors and what we believe to be true. Our belief systems drive every path and every choice we make, impulsive or not. What if you were told as a child that becoming a doctor in life is the surest way to lead a secure, happy, rich life? What if you truly believed that statement even though you were madly drawn to arts and music? Therefore, for a decade of your early adult life, you go to college, study like mad to pass the MCAT, go to medical school, and finish your residency, only to wake up one morning with this empty feeling inside.

You wanted security and a rich life, you didn't want to be a doctor, but you believed that in order to achieve security and wealth, this was your path. There is dissonance in your heart because you pushed aside all the things that filled your soul in order to stay this course that you believed would bring you security and wealth. Sure, you may have security and wealth, but you don't have the fulfillment your heart intended for you to have …

Finding Purpose

STEP 3 on Getting Clear: ***Find your purpose.*** Decide on what you want to **become** rather than what you want. This gives your desired results purpose.

STEP 4 on Getting Clear: ***Identify the fear associated with your desires and learn to transcend them.*** The desire to overcome your fears will drive you to reach your goals. If you are not willing to face your fears, it will drive you away.

Our life, careers, relationships and everything surrounding us is a direct reflection of what we choose to believe about what it means to have that in our lives. To understand our own belief systems, get clarity on what we truly want, and decide who we truly are, follow the next steps. Take time alone for yourself and truly decide on the answers. The questions are simple and it shouldn't take long, however, if you can honestly answer these questions properly and trust yourself with the answers, you will reveal some powerful, astonishing insights about yourself, which in turn will guide you to find clarity. It's best to answer quickly and precisely without over-thinking it.

1. Decide what you want to **become** rather that what you **want**. (It's best to keep this part as general as possible and list as many as you can that come to mind.)

   Example: I want to **become** a reputable person in my community, a passionate public speaker, a genuine, honest friend, a loving parent who spends quality time with my children, a well known dancer, someone who makes a difference in the lives of children, etc., etc. (don't be shy here).

I want to **become**: ______________________________

____

2. Next to each answer above, answer **why, along with the feeling it brings.**

   Example: I want to **become** a *reputable person in my community* because it (**why**) *gives me purpose, freedom, and challenge* and I **feel (feeling)** *worthy.*

   Fill in the blank: I want to **become** a ______________ because it **(why)** ______________________ and I **feel (feeling)** ______________________.

   Fill out this sentence as many times as you need to with each item from your answer to number 1.

3. Define the **FEAR** that you may feel if you do not achieve your **why.**

   Example: If I don't have (**why**) *purpose, freedom, and challenge in life, I* **(fear)** ***I*** *will be lost, trapped, constricted, bored or overworked.*

   Fill in the blanks:

   If I don't have **(why)**______________________________,

   I (**fear**)______________________________

4. List all the whys and feelings you stated above in number 2. And list all your fears you stated in number 3. For example:

   WHYS: Purpose, Freedom, Challenge

   FEELINGS: Worthy

   FEARS: Lost, Trapped, Constricted, Overworked

WHYS:____
FEELINGS: ____________________________________
FEARS: ____

The whys, feelings, and fears you list here are the beliefs about yourself that drive your being. If you filled this out correctly, you will notice a definite pattern in each column. They are your innermost desires and fears. Your whys are what you want in life. Your feelings and fears are what drive you. Now view your current lifestyle and ask this question: "Is my life designed to face the fears that I listed above, or is it designed to run away?"

STEP 3 on Getting Clear: ***Find your purpose.*** Decide on what you want to **become** rather than what you want. This gives your desired results purpose.

STEP 4 on Getting Clear: ***Identify the fear associated with your desires and learn to transcend them.***

The way you feel about something or the fear it entails are powerful driving forces of our actions and choices.

What Do You Want? Make a List … Own it!

STEP 5 on Getting Clear: *Smile and start making a long list of everything you deserve.* Keep going until you can't write anymore.

As the Dali Lama says, "Approach love and cooking with reckless abandon." We say, "Approach your list the same way!" You'll be amazed at how freeing this is … Tell yourself that you deserve wonderful, great things in life provided that you are willing to give back wonderful, great things in life.

Remember Your Five Steps

STEP 1 on Getting Clear: ***Slow down and clear your mind.***

STEP 2 on Getting Clear: ***Define your "whys" behind what you are seeking.***

STEP 3 on Getting Clear: ***Find your purpose.***

STEP 4 on Getting Clear: ***Identify the fear associated with your desires; learn to transcend them.***

Step 5 on Getting Clear: ***Smile and start making a long list of everything you deserve.***

Putting together a list of dreams and goals that mean everything to you begins to create the roadmap for all decisions going forward. You owe this to your future self.

When you give, you'll always get. Therefore, *getting* clear on your goals means *giving* the appropriate time to yourself to discover and *get* the appropriate path that is right for you.

Question number one: "How clear are you on what you want?"

Checkout Line

Michell

In finding the answer to the first question, it's important to weigh and measure the consequences of what we are asking for. The process of shopping is like a dance. The world inside a store is magical. Inside we can have, handle, try on or just carry around in our carts anything we want. We are greeted with overwhelming offers of "can I help you?" and an endless supply of attentive store clerks who will eagerly work to make us happy.

What is interesting about the checkout line is that is it the moment of ultimate decision, the time we look at our choices and actually commit to them … or not. This is the moment of truth; when the price gets paid and we take with us the items we decided on. But sometimes by the time we get to the checkout line the item's lost its appeal. "Owning it" for the time we were in the store was fulfilling enough!

We do this with life choices too; at one moment so sure of what we want next, and then sometimes even the next day completely unsure again.

The simple act of filling up the cart is almost more enjoyable than walking out of the store with the items we choose, just like dreaming and then actually committing.

Shopping "Therapy"

The experience of finding something that provided value, or would bring happiness to me or someone in my life, was easy to find through shopping "therapy." Often I wasn't after the items themselves, I was after the feeling that they provided or the result they would bring. Shopping made me feel successful, as is often the case, and knowing I could take care of people in my life rewarded me.

It's interesting to notice our individual "addictions." At garage sales, I always seem to come home with little antique wooden chairs. For one of my cousins, its plastic organizing bins. She's always excited to check out the bin section in every store that carries them. We are truly a funny species.

Life is like shopping. Everything we decide upon comes with a certain price. Paying the price is not the issue, understanding the price is. This is the purpose of the checkout line.

Standing in the checkout line at a store, I usually perform a last minute calculation before I leave … Did I get everything on my list? Did I miss anything? Do I still want it all? Can I afford it all? Is there anything in my cart that I didn't put there? I look at what I selected and I edit. I keep the things I really want and take the others off the belt. In life I've learned to do the same thing.

When we make certain choices it's important to be aware that we are also choosing to pay the price that comes with those choices—not only financial prices, but costs to relationships, health and wellness, dreams and happiness and time with loved ones. These are the real payments that we make through our lives.

To help ensure that our choices are on the right track we are now trained to go deeper than the first "why?" We learned this through the wisdom of the four-year-olds in this world and their commitment to the "Why?" game.

For example:

I want to work for myself.

Why?

Because of the freedom it will give me and the ability to make my own choices always.

Why?

I know how hard I will work when I'm in control of my results and I want the freedom financial security brings.

Why?

Because that will make me feel safe and secure and proud of my accomplishments, let me provide for others, travel and explore and enjoy life.

Why?

Because that will make me happy, and I need to be happy.

Why?

Because this is not a practice life, and I "suck" at everything when I'm not happy. When I am happy I can spend time enjoying my family and contributing to make others happy—to me this is the most important thing.

Why?

Because to me, that's a life well spent; I will be proud to have lived that life.

Everything boils down to an underlying driving factor.

Once you know your underlying "why?" you get to select a "how."

Pick one that carries a price you are prepared to pay. This is where you must be diligent. There are many, many ways to accomplish many, many things. Deciding which avenue is correct for you takes time and honest consideration.

Understand what you will trade for what you decide to pursue, and understand what you will give up for what you don't—your happiness depends on this.

Yes it can be confusing, and yes it can take time—that is fine. No reason to stress, just be aware; make the best decisions you know how, ask for help and go for it! Life will have many seasons ...

When I was younger and in University I had no idea what I wanted to do with my life. My mom thought I should become a lawyer (to get paid to argue) so I went to visit the few lawyers that I knew through friends,' parents and university professors. I asked each of them, "Would you choose your profession if you could do it all again?" The answers they gave me surprised me. This exercise taught me to ask those who have come before me for their wisdom so that I may learn some insight without earning it through experience myself.

Spending time with the question "How clear are you on what you want?" is one of the best investments of time you can give yourself. I'm not suggesting to become complacent, or to postpone working towards a result in order to spend time in limbo either, but I intensely mean for you to figure it out.

- What do you want?
- What makes you happy?
- What makes you happiest?
- If life could be exactly as you want it—what would that look like?

Build a relationship with your future.

It takes fierce courage to do this. Admitting what you want can be scary. There is a reason why studies show that only three percent of us actually even get this far and answer question number one. Ninety seven percent of us never do. Ninety seven percent of us do not make a decision and write down our goals; Ninety seven percent of us think it is too much work to even think about....

More people go to psychics and fortune tellers to ask what's in store for their future than people who actually decide on their future and set goals for themselves. Doesn't this seem irresponsible? Yes!

I also read once that 99 percent of all people give up on their goals before they even start. That struck me as a bit sad, and perhaps this has been the truth historically. **Accepting that this is the rule seems reckless.** We should change that statistic together. Perhaps that's the way it used to be, but with all of the education and awareness, strength and potential that exists in all of us we should "stale date" that statistic, and change it to teach the generations of the future.

The price of not going after what you want is often times higher than the price would have been to get it. This is not a practice life. A price gets paid for all choices, whether they are choices to take action or choices not to. Most prices – we can handle! Our resources are vast and our capabilities are often limitless.... Answering question number one, "How clear are you on what you want?" requires responsibility in the answer. This comes from understanding both the reward and the price of each choice, and then intelligently selecting what you really want.

I believe in crystal balls. But the crystal balls I believe in are the ones you can grow yourself—with courage and decision, awareness, and industrious work ethic. You decide what you want in the future and you work on getting it. How well your crystal balls work, at accurately seeing your future ... that all depends on you, and how you answer the Six Questions.

Question number one: "How clear are you on what you want?"

Question Number Two:

HOW COMMITTED ARE YOU TO GETTING IT?

99 percent committed is not enough.

Courage, Conviction, & Commitment

Julie

Question number two is:
"How committed are you to getting it?"

Going after a goal that we really want takes great courage, conviction, and commitment. Life can be treacherous and terrifying at times when there is too much uncertainty. It is easy to retreat when we are not clear on what we want or when we lose sight of our goals. It is easy to retreat too, when we lack the courage of our conviction. There is a physiological response to fear.

I remember the first time I felt fear, I was only six. All I could hear was my heart beating. Then I could hear my breath, so I tried to hold it but the more I held my breath, the louder my heartbeat sounded. It was so dark and so quiet that I was suddenly aware of the way my skin felt all over my body. I was hiding in the dark on a dare. I didn't know if my ears were growing bigger or if I was just becoming aware of every tiny little cricket outside. For some reason, the hair on the back of my neck started rising, I was feeling really hot as if I were about to explode, and my heart was beating louder and louder. Then I felt a sudden grasp and heard a scream and I jumped so hard that I bashed the top of my head on the bottom of the table. "TAG YOU"RE IT!" my brother screamed …

I remember that feeling with my adrenaline pumping as I went through the house in the dark. I'm not sure if I loved that exhilarating feeling, but I did know that if I really wanted something even though I was afraid, then that was what it physically felt like and what it took in order to force myself to do it, even though it was completely uncomfortable for me. In fact, it was downright scary. That event characterizes a lot of things in life that can stop us from moving forward. Commitment requires great courage.

Courage

How committed are you to getting what you want? It takes great courage to follow our heart and ask for the things in life we want or feel we deserve. I have had to do a lot of public speaking in my life. That wasn't natural or comfortable for me. In fact the first few times I felt like that six-year- old little girl hiding in the dark house. That terrifying feeling exists. But I didn't want to be bound by fear or be stopped from doing the things I loved.

There's a beautiful quote by spiritual activist, lecturer, and author of *A Course in Miracles* Marianne Williamson:

Our deepest fear is not that we are inadequate. Our deepest fear is that we are powerful beyond measure. It is our light, not our darkness that most frightens us. We ask ourselves, Who am I to be brilliant, gorgeous, talented, fabulous? Actually, who are you not to be?

Commitment to anything starts with courage. It is the willingness to push yourself out of your comfort zone. A friend of mine had a nice cushy job at a great company for many years. However, she observed everyone around her receiving raises, but never her. I listened to her complain day and night of the unfairness and that she should just be automatically recognized for her work. When the conversation was brought up that maybe she should go in and ask for a raise, her immediate reply was, "No, because then I think they will just fire me."

She was one of the most valued employees there, yet she was blinded by a fear that was debilitating her growth. She felt she had too much to lose and didn't want to push the limits.

Months went by and finally the day came where her boss asked to speak to her. She went in, and to her dismay, it was just for more work. As she was leaving, she turned back and, flat out, spoke her mind. In the absolute moment of confrontation, her boss agreed and gave her an enormous raise on the spot!

She admitted to me later that she was terrified. It was as if her body would explode, but it was such catharsis to finally let it out and obviously the result was greater than she even imagined.

Take a few moments and think to yourself,

- What are some things I would really like to do, but I am terrified to do them?

- What are some things I really would like to ask for, but I am afraid of the potential outcomes?
- What are some things that I really need to do, but I am fearful of the change?

After you have your answers, study this next diagram. I have seen this used many times over the years. The circles represent our fears that bind us within certain limits. The key is not always to erase all the small circles, but to recognize them and have the courage to push yourself out of them when the time comes. The more we can stretch ourselves, the more we can start designing the life we want.

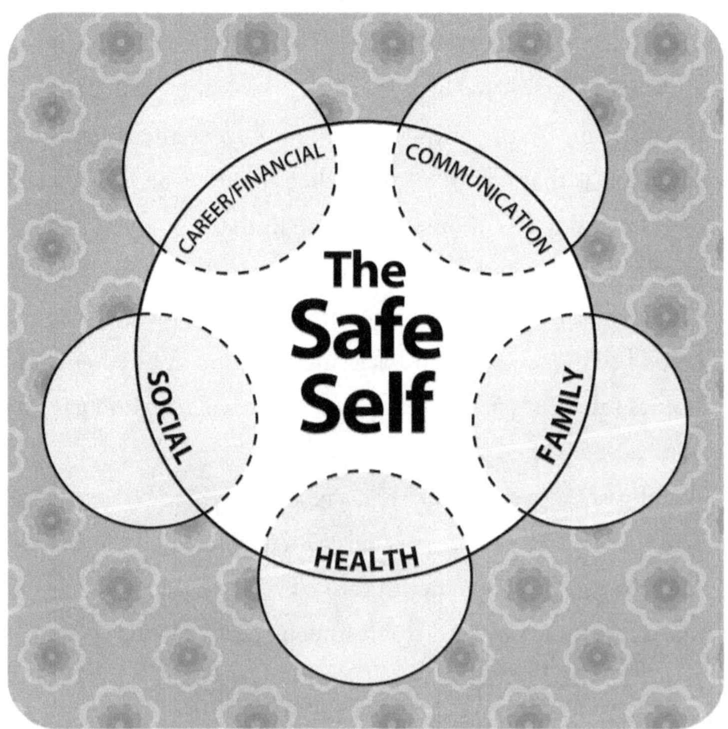

The middle of the diagram is our "safe self," where we feel most comfortable. We are surrounded in there by our safe friends and family members, our safe positions and our safe way of handling situations. This is an easy place. All the bubbles surrounding the safe self represent different areas of our lives. Each area of our life is partially inside of our comforted area and partially outside. Different situations dictate how far in and how far out each area is for us.

After college, I moved to a different city and state. I was completely outside of my comfort zone for awhile in almost every area. I didn't have any family or any close friends to lean on, had no job to report to, and barely had any money. I was terrified. This taught me courage, however uncomfortable. But my willingness to push outside of what was comfortable for me forced me to land a new position in a new market and open my own business. I could not have done that had I stayed in the comfort of the city I was in. I would never have felt the need to challenge myself then.

Sometimes, though, we are so far outside of our comfort zones that it is impossible to concentrate or reach goals, and we feel the need to retreat. Remember that having clarity on where you are going, along with courage, conviction, and commitment, can help you through those rough times.

How committed are you to getting what you want? The truest test to your commitment is your ability to transcend your fear in any area. However, remember, if you did not correctly answer question number one; "How clear are you on what you want?" then it will be close to impossible to find the courage to break through that comfort zone. There must be a driver, a goal, a purpose, or a reason. The reason could simply be to not be bound by fear. That is clear.

Conviction

Conviction is the complete belief that you can make something happen because you believe it from the bottom of your heart. One of the best examples of someone speaking with conviction was Martin Luther King's speech on "I had a dream." The conviction he spoke with was delivered with a burning desire for change and democracy. Conviction is your absolute, unwavering belief in your subject.

When the conviction is in your heart, it will fuel your courage.

Commitment

The secret to any success is the amount of commitment put forth. Commitment means not quitting when everyone around you is telling you to quit, but your heart is telling you to keep going. Commitment means not giving up when faced with the biggest of obstacles. Commitment means finding a way to work through your issues no matter what. The best way to stay committed is to remember the goal and find clarity around it once more. Keep your eye on the prize.

Becoming committed to your goals requires you to "close your back door." There's a famous story about Eric the Red, the great Viking who sailed out with only 100 of his best men in ten boats to defeat the inhabitants of an island across from their shore. Upon landing, the troops quickly realized that they were outnumbered ten to one. With already a defeated mentality and a bruised ego, the small army retreated back to their boats only to find that their leader, the great Viking, Eric, had burned their boats, leaving them no choice but to fight or die. A great, bloody battle was fought, and in the end Eric's army defeated the landowners and commandeered the island. Closing your back means leaving no other options but to hit your goal. Quitting is not an option.

This story plays out in our real lives constantly. We have too many reasons and too many places or people to retreat to; therefore it's easy for our commitment to waiver. "If Plan A doesn't work out, I can always go do Plan B." When our mentality is split between too many choices or projects, it's very difficult to commit 100 percent to one thing. This does not insinuate that you should only pursue one thing and never have a backup plan; however, the commitment level has to be at 100 percent when pursuing big changes and goals. This also means that no matter how tough the obstacles, don't lose sight of your goals. That is that "all in" concept. The term "closing your back door" precisely means that: no turning back, fight or die (metaphorically speaking, of course).

If we can find a way to live our lives passionately and commit 100 percent to the most important goals, speak with conviction about what we are going to do, and muster the courage to make it happen, we can start designing the life we want to live.

Ask yourself these six questions:

1. Am I 100 percent committed to my goal?
2. If not, what is holding me back? How can I make that 100 percent commitment?
3. What sacrifices am I willing to make in order to achieve my goal?
4. Do I believe that this can be accomplished, and can I speak with conviction about it?

5. Can I find the courage to make it happen?
6. Who can support me on this venture?

Integrity

Integrity is the key holder. When we work with integrity and uphold the highest standards for ourselves, this affects all those around us in the most positive way.

Question number two: How committed are you to getting it?

Beware the Recruiters

Michell

Waking up on the wrong side of the bed sucks. Being focused and motivated one day only to get totally discouraged the next is exhausting. Committed? Never a problem … It has always been easy to be completely committed to which ever emotion or mood decided to take control of myself and my life. Daring to stop the roller coaster and gain control in a productive and powerful way was exactly like engaging in my own private war. I won't negotiate with terrorists - my life literally depends on it.

Question number two, "How committed are you to getting it?" requires you to gain control of your mindset, in a positive way. Your commitment will get tested when you get discouraged.

Managing Our Emotions

This was a daunting concept to me when I first heard it. I had decided what I wanted to accomplish, but my commitment was at the whim of which version of myself woke up each day, and this was too risky. It was a challenge accepting the fact that I had been in control every moment, by either taking it or losing it, my whole life. The process of learning how to manage my emotions became easier when I imagined something I now call "The Wheel of Emotions."

I imagine a little circle of dancing "emoticons" all holding hands. Each one is a different version of me—an embodiment of each different emotion. One of them is always driving, always in charge, and I've permitted her to be. This helps me prevent "Evil Michell" from gaining control; "Happy Michell" makes much better choices.

Thinking of my emotions this way makes sense to me. Emotions all desperately attempt to gain control of our minds, suggesting and presenting evidence that will help them. Once they gain control, they are the most dedicated and fierce recruiters you will ever experience in any form in all of nature.

See, they do not exist unless we feel them … they are truly fighting for their lives.

Some of us have been trained to feel more comfortable holding onto negative emotions than positive ones. Several of the sayings that we even trade as common currency represent this training. "I don't want to get my hopes up"; "All good things come to an end"; etc., etc. Perhaps we even choose to be unhappy. Why? For fear of allowing happiness in "because it's only a matter of time before we will have to survive the loss of it."

It's as though we were trained as a species to be more accepting of negative beliefs and to repel positive suggestions. Strange. The whole world could use a retrain.

Negative emotions are like terrorists. They fight dirty: they set up traps, they recruit the weak and they are fully prepared to go down with the ship.

Emotions can be very dangerous. When they gain control it can feel like being intoxicated, or worse—possessed.

People in a rage are completely committed to that emotion. Rage is driving, navigating, targeting and destroying. Engaging in hostile, reactive activity with everyone it encounters, Rage is in complete control. We are not.

Once given control, all emotions are only after one thing: *keeping* control. Our emotions are all-demanding little personalities.

We all have a degree to which we allow ourselves to be emotional—an emotional volume setting of sorts. The degree to which we allow ourselves to become angered will echo the degree to which we allow ourselves to love, become sad, be excited, etc. Some of us are even turned completely off. Our emotional volume can be changed at any time by each of us; it is usually set to the level that feels right, however.

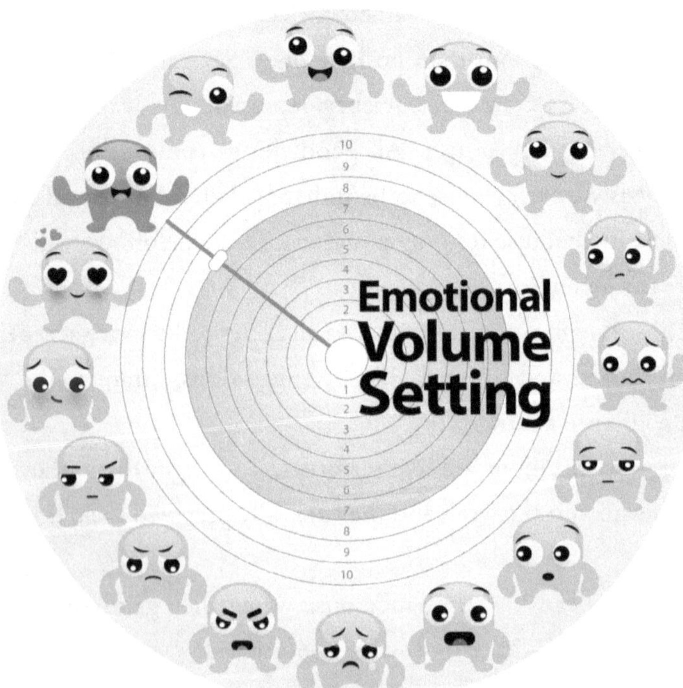

Physiologically women are hard wired to be more emotional than men. While this is a blessing in my opinion, in business it often leads to our demise. Many men are accurate in their opinion that working with women can be an emotional nightmare at times. Performance is required constantly in business, regardless of how we may feel. It is up to us to learn to control this most important part of ourselves.

We all have a "home base." That is the emotional place in which we can reside without reaction to immediate stimulus. We pick this place based on our circumstances and by the perspective we have. What we see, what we believe and what we anticipate are large contributors to how we choose to feel. Being responsible for making sure your home base is a positive place is up to you, and you must do it alone.

How committed are you?

How badly do you want what you want?

Are you prepared to work on staying positive?

Are you prepared to work on even believing that you can?

Are you perhaps prepared to do things you thought were silly, like use affirmations, morning or midnight messages, or write insurance cards for yourself?

Are you brave enough to actually try it?

I learned that I operate best when I am in my mindset zone. I do my best to keep this zone as my "home base." This is a place that is inhabited by the set of emotions that are permitted to take my wheel. Happy, excited, thoughtful, confident—all of the best versions of me are grouped together holding down one entire quarter of my emotional wheel.

I put up barriers that act as buffers to keep me within this zone as much as possible by choice. To do this I must recruit for these emotions, and I choose to do this daily. Some of these barriers are mental or internal decisions to think about the things I want to and to not think about the things I don't want to—others are barriers against certain people or negative influences in the life surrounding me.

Being aware of the emotional recruiting power in other people is also important. Beware! Spending time near people who jeopardize my mindset zone is strictly policed. People who have a negative impact on me are removed or are avoided at all costs.

Fear as a driver is common. Fear recruits in numbers and expects to survive through this strategy. Fear succeeds when we fail.

Emotions have discovered that they stand a better chance at survival if they can control people collectively. They work as a unified force that attempts to gain strength through each of us. They spread throughout all of us and operate as a single entity.

Imagine that the entire world is only comprised of the number of personalities on the emotional wheel ... and they are all competing for ultimate control. They recruit and fight to spread fear, hatred and sorrow, or love, happiness and peace ... the age old battle of good versus evil.

Each of us chooses inside ourselves which side we fight for every day of our lives, and whatever each of us thinks about, grows. We are infectious cures or infectious diseases for other people in our lives. We either bring brightness or darkness with our comments, our presence and our intentions. Emotional currency operates in a unique way; it is constantly traded every second of every moment—this market never closes.

Getting clear on what you want and being committed to getting it is an intentional decision. It requires the choice to feed the positive side of yourself and to mute the negative, doubtful side. This takes dedication. For me it took developing an entire program I called "Attitude Anonymous" to learn how to keep myself positive. Deciding to keep your hopes up even when things are tough is an indicator of your commitment level to the future you want. If your commitment wavers, what you are striving for also gets farther out of reach. But when your commitment holds—progress happens faster.

Gaining control of your emotions and choosing to be positive can change your life. Being in an honestly good mood most days is pretty incredible, and surprisingly it can happen quickly. Most of us have much more abundance in our lives than we may realize … sometimes it just takes paying more attention to see it.

Beware though, the recruiters never go to sleep, and are always … waiting.

Question number two: "How committed are you to getting it?" Only listen to the positive recruiters …

Chapter 7

PERFORMING THE EXORCISM

Michell

Committing yourself to getting what you want requires a removal of the negative energy that is stopping you from achieving your goals. Finding the right answer to question number two is fueled by this.

I agree it doesn't sound pleasant. Being stuck in the yo-yo land of the motivated and the unmotivated was even more unpleasant though, and control needed to be mine again.

I had decided what I wanted to accomplish and had begun the pursuit of this new endeavor, but I constantly flip-flopped back and forth between on-track and totally off-track. Some days I was completely in the zone; I had courage, commitment and conviction. Other days I would wake up and think "who am I kidding?" I'd focus on all of the reasons why success was next to impossible and how hard it was to even attempt to think positively. I was possessed by the doubtful, exhausted version of myself.

My motivation level constantly varied depending on my mindset and emotional state. I recognized that I was not in control of my wheel of emotions yet and was at the mercy of the negative doubters inside me whenever negative results started to show up. This would throw me farther off track and exhaust me in the fight. Being aware of what I needed to do was freeing in concept, but I recognized that I did not yet have the strength and skill to gain control. This frustrated me more than anything.

This is what I did.

I performed an exorcism. I forced myself through logic to pick a side. Doing this permitted me to win.

The Pros and the Cons

With no distractions and no time restriction, I sat down and worked it out. The first thing I did was get negative ... really negative. Using notepaper I wrote down every negative thing about my new endeavor that I had ever thought. I made a list of all of the things I didn't like about it. I wrote down all of the reasons why failure was inevitable. I wrote down all of the troublesome sacrifices I was required to make to attempt to succeed. I wrote down in detail absolutely everything I could think of as to why I should quit, and all of the work I was going to have to do, and everything I would have to give up. I really went into detail about the true cost of attempting to succeed. I fully embraced the negative doubters inside myself and committed their ranting to paper.

Then I took out another sheet of paper and wrote down the other side, the positive side. I wrote down all of the reasons I wanted to pursue this endeavor. I wrote down all of the benefits I would achieve if I succeeded. I wrote down the way that this would make me feel. I wrote down how this would affect my life. I wrote down what this would give me for the future, the help I could provide to others, the way I would feel about myself and the options I would have. I fast forwarded and pictured ultimate success at this endeavor and how dramatically this success would change everything in life. I wrote with ambition and confidence and excitement about the massiveness of the impact this would have. I put my heart on that paper with every hope and dream I had for the future that would be realized through the success of this adventure.

I drew a devil face at the top of the negative list and a happy face at the top of the positive list. I laid them side by side and I weighed them against each other for hours. I started the battle in my mind as to which side to pick, once and for all. I began with the negative side. I allowed myself to feel with complete commitment all of the reasons I should not pursue this project any further. I embraced the anger I felt for the sacrifices I would be expected to make and the ridiculous degree of commitment that would be expected. I decided and agreed that this endeavor was in fact a poor choice for all of these reasons. Besides, no one I knew was prepared to give up so much in the pursuit of success, therefore, I was probably crazy to think I could. But I didn't like how this place felt.

Then I tentatively considered the positive side. The enthusiasm that I had for the future where I won at this was undeniable, the immediate change in feeling the second I looked at the other sheet flooded through me. I wanted the life that I saw written on that paper.

I wanted that life more than I wanted anything else. I believed that I could actually attain that life through this particular business venture too. I believed I deserved to feel that way about my life and myself. I wanted to get my hopes up, and I was prepared to fight for it with every fiber in my being. No one else in my world believed that this was the right decision, except for me. I had to guarantee that I wouldn't quit on myself because I was all I had.

The challenge now became, if I resolved that I was going to fight to win, then I had to accept in this moment all of the negative pieces and sacrifices that were required to reach the positive outcome. This was not a decision to *ignore* the negative side but to *accept* it. It was part of the entire result in which I also won the things I wanted. I was in the checkout line and must decide if the price was worth it for me. I had to release my anger for that price and accept it as part of the package. By accepting the price, I exorcised the negative doubters and never allowed the challenges again to discourage me from the pursuit of progress. I accepted the sacrifices with intention, I embraced them, and I no longer would allow them to prevent me from staying focused. I decided that the reward was worth the risk and the cost. Now, all that mattered was whether or not I believed in my ability to succeed at the challenge.

For me, gaining clarity through the emotional haze is necessary to make smart decisions. Any time now when I find myself on the teeter totter of progress, I go through this process.

Writing down on paper the two sides which seem to be waging war inside of me, and all of their arguments is almost like giving them their day in court. All evidence is examined and each side is completely exposed.

Then I decide. I reach a verdict. I choose. I completely commit. One side wins, the other is silenced.

Reaching your goals and living the life you want should be non-negotiable too. However many exorcisms we'll have to perform along the way should also be irrelevant.

Are you clear on what you want? Are you committed to getting it? Then don't let anything stop you … most of all, you.

Question Number Three:

How Do You See Yourself?

How we see ourselves affects every single thing in our worlds.

Chapter 8:
Mirror, Mirror on the Wall

Chapter 9:
Construction Zone

Chapter 10:
Lock and Load

Chapter 8

MIRROR, MIRROR ON THE WALL…

Julie

Question number three is:
"How do you see yourself?"

The concept of "through the looking glass" is the truest representation of the world we all see. The reflection we choose to see is what shapes our decisions, our perceptions of others and essentially our lives. It drives the way we think. Our reflection is based on emotions, past experiences, past traumas and past pleasurable experiences. Our interpretations of the things that were happening at different times in our life dictate our judgment of the eyes looking back at us. Sometimes we see ourselves as tired, unhappy, challenged, older, or scared. Sometimes we see ourselves as beautiful, wise, happy, glowing, successful and dynamic. Sometimes, it depends on the angle. **How do you see yourself?**

A lot of the things we see are masks hiding our self-doubt or low self-esteem; it's our ego projecting a false larger image of who we are because of feelings of inadequacy. Reality is, when you see yourself in its purest most honest form, your reflection is most beautiful and most free. When you are able to remove the masks, face and transcend your fears, and see yourself as confident, capable, and lovable, you are able to move on to the next question. Question number three is **"How do you see yourself?"**

Self-help advocate, author, and lecturer, Dr. Wayne Dyer usually advises,

Change the way you look at things and the things you look at change.

It's actually freeing to feel and to think that we can actually alter our surroundings and change the way people respond to us just by changing the way we see our own reflection. It is also freeing to know that we do have control over our emotions, our present situation and our future outcomes. It is most freeing to know that we don't have to accept our current environment for what it is.

- We have what we have because that is what we've worked for.
- We have what we have because of the way we think about ourselves.
- The people around us treat us the way we teach them to treat us.
- We manage ourselves.
- We are accountable for our own results. This taught me to invest in failure.
- **How do you see yourself?**

A Friend from the Past … and a Puzzle

When I was in my late twenties, my business was at an all time high and I was feeling really great about my accomplishments and my personal growth. A long-time friend of mine contacted me one day; she was having a lot of difficulty in her life. She was in a financial hole and was having a really hard time with her mother, so I asked her to hang out with me for the weekend. The issue with her though, was that she never ever had any money. It seemed that was always her biggest complaint.

As long as I knew her, which was a couple decades by then, she always felt as though she didn't have anything regardless of how much she made.

Ten years earlier, I had come to realize that it was our perception of what we could do with what we had, that altered the way we made all our decisions. Money was really tight back then. If I had fifty dollars in my pocket and I spent it on one designer lipstick with a case which I would probably lose within the next 30 days, I would set myself up to feel as though, no matter how hard I worked, I could not get ahead. This thought would lead me to resent my job and convince myself that I never had money. But when the basic necessities are not met, luxury items can be trouble. Then someone taught me to always think about all the things I could do with $50 if I changed my perception of what I could do with it. So instead, I started appreciating the worth of $50 and viewed it as having a lot and I quickly realized how far I could stretch that amount. It changed the way I felt about myself and the way I viewed money. It changed my reflection. The way I saw myself changed.

Return now to my late twenties when my long-time friend called me. She was in desperate straits, asking for help, which I always graciously gave in return for all the great emotional and social support she gave me all the years I'd known her. When the weekend ended and she was leaving my condo, she looked around and looked at me and said, "You know, you are so lucky. You have always been so lucky. As long as I've known you, things seem to always go your way. You always are successful, and you always seem to have everything."

Later that afternoon when I was alone, I thought about those statements my friend made. She was beautiful, intelligent, extremely likable and always kind. Why would she assume that success is just good luck? Was her reflection of herself so different from what I was seeing when I looked at her? Did she honestly think that she couldn't have great things in her life unless someone appeared and handed her that golden ticket? In my opinion, I thought she was one of the most fascinating people I'd ever met. However, that is not what her reflection told her.

I never considered myself randomly lucky. In fact, I knew that wasn't the case. Everyone experiences random acts of luck and misfortune; however we create our own outcomes, good or bad, based on our perceptions that in turn create our actions. The "luck" is just a basic reaction to our actions. Sure, I expect the best to happen, and sure, my outlook in life can be eternally optimistic, but it really starts with the *perception* of what we *believe* we can do with what we *have* that first creates our environment. **How do you see yourself?**

Our perception of what we can do with what we have and how we see ourselves alters the way we make all our decisions.

After having interviewed over 25,000 people now in my career and having worked with thousands, I realize that there are two extreme ways we can see ourself. One is where we have no control over our thoughts, i.e., a victim mentality, creating a prisoner affect of our own mind. The other extreme (and much more positive) attitude is assuming full accountability and creativity, where we take full responsibility for results, good and bad. I have experienced both extremes.

Seeing Yourself as the Prisoner

The first extreme is the mindset where we **see** ourselves as the prisoner. We feel as though nothing is going the right way, no one is paying attention, the people around us are completely incompetent or helpless, they don't care, we can't trust anyone, everyone is in our way, everyone is irresponsible and unreliable, the system is working against us or conspiring against us, and or someone is out to get us. This could be directed at a company, a system, a team of people, a particular person, the weather, the cars on the road, our boss or team leader, our clients, our employees, the clerk behind the counter, the air conditioner guy, our household pet, or anyone or anything that we feel is stopping us from something, overcharging us for something, or completely inconveniencing us. We **see** ourselves in everyone else's problems rather than looking inside.

This is the *blaming principle*, and it exists within all of us at times. It is a helpless perception with a helpless reflection. We are a prisoner of our own circumstances. We are running from our own reflection in hopes that someone else can take responsibility for what is not right in our life.

No doubt everyone has misfortunes, faces challenging situations, unfair incidents, and difficult people in their life at times. However, seeing ourselves as a prisoner in this pattern can be destructive and lead to burn-out and frustration, and it can cause an unhappy and unhealthy environment for everyone surrounding us. It also leads to anger and depression.

Those operating at this extreme make statements like,

- No one cares.
- That person gets special treatment.

- I can't rely on anyone, so I have to do it myself,
- I don't trust him.
- They are all judging me.
- They always blame me.
- I give and get nothing back.
- No one understands and no one cares.
- There is a lot of favoritism here.
- This is so unfair.
- It's a damned if I do, damned if I don't situation.
- I am being targeted. They set me up to fail.

This person is the victim. Usually the people that get the blame are the people we love the most, the ones that we work closest with, our supervisors, or anyone we think may have some type of say so or influence in our life.

There is truth to the statement that we can't control our circumstances or surroundings or the people around us, but we can control our mindset, our emotions, our approach and our perspective. **How do you see yourself?**

Seeing Yourself as the Victor

The other extreme is **seeing** us as the victor. It's the creative place where we can clearly internalize all of our surroundings, think through options, and take full accountability for our mishaps and enjoy any success without fear that it is only a stroke of good luck. This requires confidence, patience, and an ability to see the other person's point of view. When the smallest or the largest of circumstances are not reaching our expectations, we take accountability for the results and think through the actions that need to be changed in order to get a different and, hopefully, desired result. It means that we are going to view the situation, circumstance, behavior, or result and ask ourselves these questions:

- What can I do moving forward to get a different result than what is currently happening?
- If I was in the persons shoes, what would I have done?
- How can I approach this person or team without blame, to get a different result?
- Maybe I am the one that is causing the issue?
- What responsible actions can I take or what other people can I delegate to?
- I hold myself accountable for the team not getting the work done. What is my next step?
- What things can I control and what can I do moving forward?
- Where do I have to change my focus?
- I need to stop making assumptions about the person or circumstance and think to myself, what else did they mean?

A notable example of an extremely fearless woman is tennis pro Billie Jean King. She changed the lives of other female tennis players. In 1967, she was selected as "Outstanding Female Athlete of the World." In 1972, she was named *Sports Illustrated*'s "Sportsperson of the Year," the first woman to be so honored; and in 1973, she was dubbed "Female Athlete of the Year." She was the first female athlete to win over $100,000 in prize money in a single season.

Billie Jean King lived through a time where women were not paid the same as men in sports, were not treated equally and definitely were not viewed as world champions. Instead of blaming the system and accepting the undesirable results, she spoke out for women and their right to earn comparable money in tennis and other sports. Her constant lobbying and commitments have broken many barriers. For her contributions to tennis as President of Tennis-America, she was awarded the National Service Bowl.

Billie Jean King is amongst an elite group of athletes and her mentality was that of an extreme no-excuse, victor type of person. In our lives, however the take-charge examples don't have to be so extreme. The real fact is, that we all exhibit these characteristics and traits, just in different situations; it's just how far down the line it exists for each of us.

Using the diagram below think of a current situation where you are feeling conflict and mark on the scale where you see yourself. This varies dependent on each situation and person. Are you thinking through solutions and the things you can control? Or are you trying to escape the anger by finding instant relief in blaming someone else? Sometimes we try to find instant escape as well by thinking that someone else can solve all of our issues. That is not taking responsibility for your actions. That is simply redirecting your responsibility onto someone else.

*** *** *** ***

The Prisoner The Victor

How do you see yourself? Are you the prisoner or the victor? **It takes a lot of courage to look in the mirror.** Taking responsibility for your own situation can be very difficult and require hard work and new thought patterns. Making difficult decisions is "just plain heavy" sometimes. In the short term, it can feel like the easier choice is to not take personal responsibility.

The "woe is me" concept may feel good for a moment and it's easy to do; however, no one likes to be around that type of behavior for long periods of time. It's time to look in the mirror and see a different reflection.

Empowering thoughts:

I am only responsible for my own emotions and my own circumstances. I can't control anyone else. I can only control myself. I take responsibility when things are not in my favor.

When feeling like the prisoner or where your expectations are not being met, ask yourself these questions:

"What can I do about it?"

"How can I resolve this?"

"I can't change others, but I can change myself. How can I change myself or my approach, so that others will change the way they treat me?"

"The relationship has to work, I have to make this happen. What are my next steps?"

"What's the solution?"

"Is it really true what I'm thinking or did I make it up or overreact?"

"Is there another solution?"

"What can I do, or what can I say to find a solution or change the behavior?"

Remember the old myth, "The grass is greener on the other side." Looking to someone else to escape your own issues with your current relationships or situations is only redirecting your problem somewhere else.

Think of it this way. If you are taking a class and you cannot relate to the teacher, you still have to pass the class regardless of how the information is being taught.

- If you fail a class, do you blame the teacher?
- If you get a speeding ticket, do you blame the police officer?
- If you stub your toe, do you blame the furniture or the universe?
- If your perfectly trainable pet continues to do his business on your living room floor, is it your pet's fault?
- If you are late to work, do you blame the traffic?
- If you have several failed relationships, were they *all* wrong?
- Do you think there is some big, black, dark angel of fate that is trying to make your life terrible?

We are a result of all the things we've learned, heard, felt and experienced from the day we were born. It was also largely how we interpreted our surroundings that lay our foundation.

The reflection that we see in the world around us is a projection from the world within us.

Simply put, it's not the dress; it's the girl in the dress.

Question number three: How do you see yourself?

Chapter 9

Construction Zone

Michell

When answering question number three: "How do you see yourself?" it's important to understand what drives your own belief system.

One of the biggest and most difficult lessons I ever took the time to hear, consider, disagree with, and then finally surrender to and actually digest, was that "you must take 100 percent responsibility for everything that exists in your life." It is only in accepting this responsibility that we start to ask questions. In asking these questions we start to find answers. I resisted this because I didn't want to be responsible. I thought it was easier to blame others for unhappy results. I was wrong. It wasn't easy at all to be unhappy "with good reason," in fact, it "sucked."

There are a few truths to accept about this process:

- Having a happy and successful future is not a *goal* it is a *result.* It is a result of the tiny choices we make every day.
- All changes make an impact; even the tiniest changes in thinking sometimes carry the biggest results.

I've learned to repeatedly question my faith. Not faith in a religious sense but faith in what I believe about myself to be true. I was confronted with this for the first time in my twenties. It was when I was learning to run a business, and I resisted learning about finances because it "gave me a headache," even at the suggestion of looking at numbers.

To Do Math, or Not To Do Math …

I believed that "I can't do math." My coaches at the time refused to allow me to delegate this part of my learning and forced me to ask myself a tough question—why? Why did I resist math. Why did I feel a lack of confidence in myself when engaged in financial activities? Why did I believe I wasn't capable of doing it? The answer freed me.

> *In grade school I was selected to be part of a new experimental accelerated learning program. When I was in grade seven I went through some testing in school with a group of my classmates (as many of us did).*
>
> *I was selected with five other students to become part of a "new" enriched learning program. What they did was this …*
>
> *They decided that it would help us to completely skip grade eight math and go directly into an advanced grade nine Math class instead. The six of us were bussed every day to our local high school. We were inserted into the grade*

nine enriched math class as twelve year olds with the highly advanced fourteen year olds. We were tiny, scared, intimidated and resented by the fourteen year olds, all in an instant of showing up.

Day one of class began and I, for one, was completely lost. For the first time in my scholastic career—I really doubted myself. I felt dumb and insecure. I am certain this was not the goal, it was however the result. I began to build several beliefs about myself which were not positive beliefs. "I can't do math" was the biggest one, "I don't care" was how I survived it. Every time the teacher taught a lesson that went over my head I thought "I can't do this." Every time I couldn't do my homework I thought "I can't do this." Every time I failed a test I thought "I can't do this." Because I did not know how to fix it, "I don't care" as a conviction, grew just as strong.

This was a terrible experience and it lasted for two years. Barely passing grade nine math and again barely squeaking through grade ten math, I divorced this subject the first opportunity that I was allowed to. At that moment—at fourteen years of age—I decided that whatever I wanted to do with my life, it would have nothing to do with math or science, and I dropped both subjects out of my world.

I had made a decision about what I thought about myself, and permitted that opinion to be law, until I changed it. Discovering that this belief was created by the twelve-year-old version of me made me understand an incredible truth about many of us as adults … we are prisoners of the opinions of ourselves as children. We carry with us "truths" that were created by uneducated, inexperienced, socially conflicted, insecure kids.

This experience opened a door: it freed me to challenge everything I believed about myself and gave me permission to redesign my life "with intention."

Today I think of myself exactly as I think of a computer. My mind runs software programs that I have uploaded throughout my life. Some of the programs are viruses that somehow got in there when my firewalls were down. Some are old programs that are severely out of date and they slow down my ability to process new tasks so they must be removed.

Programming is a constant in and throughout our lives. It started when our lives began and is a never-ending stream of cause and effect, investigation and awakening, deduction and discovery. And throughout our lives there are many different programmers who have influenced us. Starting at the beginning, as a child, our programmers were mostly our parents or grandparents, other relatives and caregivers, our teachers and perhaps neighbors. They all played an influential role. Their beliefs and opinions helped form our beliefs and opinions and became the foundation stones from which we've built the rest of our lives.

As an older child, many of the same people continued programming us, and some new friends were added to that programmer list. Throughout our lives, not only do we draw conclusions about ourselves with the experience of a school child, but we draw all kinds of conclusions based on the opinions of all the other school kids too ... messy!

Often in school we have our first experience facing social disapproval or rejection from our peers, and this is almost always leaves a painful and life-altering emotional scar, certainly one we never forget. Great life lessons we learned from terrified ten-year-olds. It's a wonder that we survive the growing up process at all …

As a teenager our programmers, in general, dramatically change. They are now dominantly our friends and peers, perhaps a teacher or athletic coach, maybe an older sibling or mentor; and in most cases the influence of our parents has lessened. We make crazy decisions to gain social approval and do things we would never consider doing without an audience.

As an adult, my primary programmer ***should be me.*** I should consciously choose which programs to keep and which ones to delete. It's the same as choosing which beliefs to keep and which ones to demolish. When I was introduced to this concept I was undeniably excited. I started my renovation by asking myself two questions:

1. **What do I believe about myself to be true?**
2. **What do I want to believe about myself to be true?**

It struck me that almost all of us have gotten into arguments with someone we care about over something that we made ourselves believe—that simply was not real, and we possibly even damaged the relationship because of it.

Perhaps I had built inaccurate beliefs about myself that were equally untrue and harmful, and the relationship that I had with myself had also suffered from this misguided practice. It was time to change that. I know I must be careful which side of the coin I choose to fight for—because I will win … either way. Deciding what I wanted to believe first was necessary. I made a list of my beliefs, and decided which ones to keep and which ones to eliminate.

Removing any of the beliefs I didn't like was in some cases as simple as deciding not to believe them anymore. In other cases it was disproving them by building opposite beliefs and by their existence alone they eventually eliminated the previous ones.

I learned to think of my beliefs as my own personal city skyline. Each belief, like a building, stands as tall as I've chosen to build it, and all of the beliefs I have, fill this skyline by my design.

This skyline looks different (just as real ones do) throughout the stages of my life. Old buildings were knocked down sometimes with intention and were replaced by new ones; some were renovated and some were abandoned. Some of them were knocked down by an explosion or negative experience that affected me in a negative way and made me question myself. Just as in a real construction zone, digging down and building the solid foundation for new beliefs always takes longer than building a solid belief, tall on that foundation.

When I started out in the business world I believed that things would be different for me as a woman. My behavior, however, was altered in order to compensate for this belief, and, without realizing it, it was the biggest obstacle to me succeeding. For as long as I saw things as different for a woman, so would others around me.

Eliminating old beliefs and deleting old programming for me preceded the freedom required to begin building new beliefs and making room for new programming. How we see ourselves affects every single thing in our respective worlds. We must see someone we believe in and are proud of.

This was the process I went through, and the following four steps I advise others to follow if they are looking to find the same freedom:

Step 1: Pack Your Dynamite

Eliminate your negative beliefs no matter how long you've had them or how you "know they're true." It's time to leave **here** and get **there**. Eliminate your negative beliefs or you will fail to make the desired change.

The easiest way to eliminate an old belief is to create a new one that disproves the old one. Take for example my experience with math. In order to build a new belief called "I can do math," I simply paid attention and looked for evidence to prove this to be true. Every time I placed a foundation stone under the new belief, it removed one from the old belief and soon I had disproved the old one.

Just because for the first half of our lives things were a certain way does not mean they will stay that way for the rest of our lives. We need to build enough proof to support our new beliefs more strongly than the old ones were supported. Just as lawyers build a case in a court of law, we build a case in the courtroom of our minds. But *we* get to decide which case to build. It is not up to anyone else.

Step 2: Fire Your Insecurities

All of the reasons you've trained your brain to recite to you as to why making these changes will be difficult—REMOVE THOSE VOICES from your "advisory board."

Refusing to listen to negative messaging is also your exclusive responsibility. Talk to yourself out loud, listen to tapes, do whatever you need to do to drown out those voices. This step is not optional.

Step 3: Change the Channel

The voice that's broadcasting in your head **already** about whether or not this will work … if it's saying anything negative, change the channel. You do it with the radio all the time … do it with yourself.

Step 4: Close the Recruiting Centre

No longer look for or listen to any proof that these negative beliefs are true. Just stop it. When companies are hiring for a certain position they do not take on people for positions that are un-needed. Neither should you.

Step 5: Let Yourself Off the Hook

Thinking of our previous failures only serves us in the lessons we learn. Keep the lessons but let go of the blame. Know your intentions were good and you're doing your best. Let the bad stuff go!

Step 6: Delete Old Programming

The things you used to believe about yourself that held you back and limited your performance: highlight them and hit the delete button. That's it. Gone... Bye-bye.

Step 7: Empty the Recycle Bin.

Seriously ... get rid of it ... let it go.

Question number three: How do you see yourself?

This affects EVERYTHING else in your world. **What do you want to believe?**

Chapter 10

LOCK AND LOAD

Michell

To see yourself as confident, successful and free requires new thought patterns. **How do you see yourself? Time to choose …**

Liking who you are is required. Harnessing the power of the X Factor (for the ladies, and the "Y" factor for the men) happens right here—in this space. Spending time to give yourself credit and permission to feel good builds your genuine confidence, fills you with the good kind of pride. This confidence and pride become your protective wear, like armor or Teflon, a force field … it's like putting on an impenetrable helmet. Deciding what to build next in life when you're protected is an exciting prospect.

The beauty of being a helmet nerd is truly magnificent. Helmets allow adventure to be a regular part of life, and living becomes something we do with intention. Life is way more fun to live if we're prepared to live life in the fast lane.

Generally speaking, men have tougher armor than women. It starts from the time we were all kids and men rough-housed while we had tea parties. Men played street hockey and got stitches while we had sleepover parties and braided each other's hair. Even for those of us who were tomboys as little girls, the degree of toughness is still different … the world tends to treat little girls as though we might break. Learning to be strong is required.

Building the life that you want requires certain tools and they can only be purchased through sweat equity and mental toughness; their currency is one of a higher kind.

This is not a practice life; you get one "go 'round," and adventure awaits, so—buckle up, buttercup.

Deciding how you see yourself is your responsibility. Becoming the person you want to be starts with a decision to do so. Developing the skills and habits you need to support this new "you" are more easily achieved by following eight basic guidelines:

1. Learn to Lengthen Your Fuse

Storms will arrive in each of our lives. Choosing to navigate them instead of running from them completely changes the game. Expecting things to go wrong, (though not in a foreboding kind of way), is freeing.

We don't go down that easy … and even if we do—try and make us stay there … Treating problems as though they are normal takes their power away. We are all pretty incredible and capable people.

I remember my first experience with a school bully. I was eight years old. I was terrified of getting selected as her next victim and therefore learned to fly under the radar when she was around. But … my turn eventually came. I do not remember the circumstances or the words or anything else about it except my reaction.

I immediately collapsed into tears and ran home to my mom and never wanted to go back to school again. The depth of the wound that this experience left on me forced future conflict to be met differently.

All of us are taught to take one of two stances when we are faced with challenge or adversity in grade school—stand up for ourselves or get bullied. I remember the insurmountable fear that existed when I started to learn to stand up for myself. I learned that the faster I talked back and the louder and stronger my voice, the more convincing I was as an equal threat. I even learned to walk around with a face on that said "don't mess with me" loud and clear to everyone who looked at it. (I see this face on teenagers all the time and I understand why they wear it.) I too spent my teenage years with my offensive players on the field all the time.

This worked as a child and is a juvenile response to conflict. While this was effective in the school yard at recess it needs to be reprogrammed as an adult. We all know adults in our lives that still react like children. It's the only way they ever learned to deal with conflict.

Our ability to remain calm when facing challenge, disappointment or adversity is the biggest contributing factor to progress. High performance people do not lose time because they've lost their cool. Learning to skip the "emotional response" part and move directly to the "What do we do now?" part is the mission critical to navigating through life. Any way we look at it, we cannot change things after they have occurred. The amount of time we spend sending ourselves to our own emotional "penalty box" is precious time wasted out of the game.

2. Increase Your Tolerance for Trouble

During life's critical moments when a severe bodily injury occurs, our trained reaction is to call 911. We call the people who are trained and capable of handling life-threatening injuries. They are calm and efficient and undeniable heroes. During life's critical moments when other severe challenges occur, we need to be able to count on ourselves to be calm and efficient heroes.

Having a high tolerance means that it takes A LOT to affect us. We don't get fazed by much, we keep our cool. To be proud of being a great problem solver means we're going to have to face lots of problems to solve. Remaining calm when the stakes are high is the only way to continue to make clear and rational decisions. Throwing ourselves off an emotional cliff because something went wrong ends the game.

3. Develop Your Patience

Things take time. Deadlines get pushed back. Deliveries get postponed. People re-prioritize.

Getting angry doesn't change this.

Getting frustrated never helps us either.

4. Expect to Succeed—Success Is a Mindset

Confidence and action are a very powerful tag team. They follow the lead your expectations provide. What you see in the future determines what you see in the present – the truest example of "what you see is what you get."

5. Ask for Confirmation only from Within

The only person who has to believe these beliefs is you. Looking to find validation in others is a risky experiment. Most of the time what others will give you, unfortunately, is doubt with very few exceptions. Playing *Jenga* with your beliefs is unwise.

Close your eyes and ask yourself how you feel. If what you're doing feels right, then embrace it. Say out loud so that you can hear the confidence in your own voice "I can do this," and allow the feeling of confidence to stay with you ... your little secret wing woman.

6. Build on What You Already Know

Lean on the foundational beliefs that you already have about yourself. You are strong. You have integrity. You choose to do the right thing not the easy thing. You can do this too. Any of the past beliefs that make you proud, that build you up—use these to support the new beliefs until they have enough evidence on their own. Bridge your beliefs the same way you learned to build with Lego. You could build as tall and as creatively as your mind allowed as long as you had solid supporting walls to carry the weight of the design.

I learned to drive standard as a teenager which at the time I thought was another way my parents opted to torture me instead of just buying a new family car that was automatic.

One overly dramatic afternoon filled with panic, doubt and fear, my mom taught me an incredible lesson. We had pulled over at the side of the road near the beach in Toronto.

The road we were on was on an incline and I had to get the car to start without rolling back. She was teaching

> *me to balance the clutch in the toughest scenario possible so that once I'd mastered this I would be able to do this always.*
>
> *I had spent the morning successfully driving (kind of) on pretty flat roads but was truly afraid of how steep roads changed the game. I stalled the car and panicked. I was humiliated as I was blocking traffic, so of course I got angry at my mom for making me do this.*
>
> *My mom turned on the flashers, kept her hand securely on the emergency brake and calmly told me to relax. "Who cares what anybody else is thinking right now. You can do this, you just have to feel the car and do what you know how to do. You have been doing this all morning on flat roads. The roads do not decide if you can operate this car or not. You do. This is not any different."*
>
> *Stealing some confidence from the look in her eyes and allowing me to feel like the girl she saw in front of her, I did calm down and I did get up that hill.*

Overcoming that one incredible fear and comprehending the depth of the lesson behind it was a life changing day for me. Certainly not at the time was I able to understand this, but on reflection, my mother did more than teach me how to drive standard up a hill that day. She taught me that regardless of the terrain, you can overcome.

How many times in business have I taken a stand only to receive negative feedback with an audience? Well I just put my parking brake on then too and took the time required to handle things the right way instead of the fast way in a panic.

You just need to stay calm and build on what you already know.

7. Commit to the Person You Are Becoming

Behave in the way required to support these new beliefs. Reprogramming behaviors takes time. Put effort into behaving the way you need to behave to create the person you want to become.

Fairly early in my career I was asked to speak at a conference for sales managers. There were to be over a thousand attendees in the audience—most of whom were older than me and more experienced. I had found some early success through unbelievable sacrifice and work ethic and was told that I could teach them some things even though I had less experience. I was terrified.

Not only did I have a fear of speaking in front of this many people—I never had before—but I also was aware that my presence might be met with some cynical resistance by my more experienced peers.

I had a decision to make: either just get through it or write the best speech I could write and attempt to win the respect of the room by actually delivering.

When I ran up to the podium at the beginning of my speech I could feel the mixed reception in the room. I had some fans who knew my intent was genuine and my desire was to simply help if I could, and then there were all the others who were either indifferent or judging me before I began.

I decided to go for it right from the beginning, and started my speech with "I believe you have to have balls to run a business, and it's clear to me that not enough people in this room actually do."

That silenced the entire room.

And the tap-dance began … I went through my topic, discussing that truly being committed to your business, the people working with you and your collective success means being honest about what you are working towards and demanding 100 percent of yourself first.

When you knew that you yourself were "all in" you generally could incite that in the performance of others around you. I believe that with this one change the entire minutia goes away and success starts to show up more readily. I talked about growing crystal balls …

My intent was to inspire people to believe in themselves. Not in me, not in a business model—in themselves. To stop caring whether or not other people thought they were successful and actually just accomplishing it, if they could. When people are sure about where they're going and eliminate the doubt in themselves—success pays attention.

This speech was my first big test. I got a standing ovation from the entire room … the only one out of thirty speakers.

8. Discipline Gets You There

Find some time every week even if it's just for a few minutes to check in with your beliefs. Perhaps it is in the morning over coffee, on your lunch break or when the kids are finally asleep!

Write down the beliefs you are creating. Record every piece of evidence you encounter to support these beliefs. Close your eyes and allow yourself to feel these new beliefs. Pat yourself on the back and feel proud of yourself for just five minutes. Allowing and encouraging this feeling to exist is the only way it will …

How you see yourself matters more than anything else. True strength grows *here*. True strength is unbreakable.

Question number three: How do you see yourself?

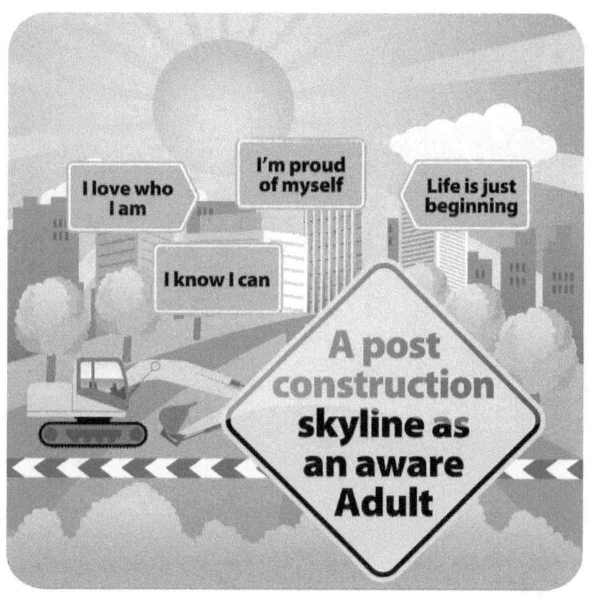

For more tips on presenting the confident person you are, visit us at **www.JulieandMichell.com**

Question Number Four:

HOW ARE YOU MANAGING YOUR SURROUNDINGS?

Relationships, circumstances, obstacles, and successes are not accidental.

Chapter 11

WHO'S AT YOUR PARTY?

Julie

Question number four is:
"How are you managing your surroundings?"

Managing your surroundings is a huge step in gaining control of your path. In order to understand how to manage your surroundings, it's important to first realize all the people in your life and the parts they play. Do you ever question why certain situations and people are in your life? Do you ever wish there were more of certain types of people in your life?

Understanding and emotionally managing your relationships gives you sense of peace, aids in building your confidence, and clears your path for massive growth in every area of your life. This does not mean controlling or managing others, this means controlling and managing your own emotions and understanding the part everyone plays in your life.

Relationships are not accidental.

If your life is a party, your favorite type of party, whatever that might be, who's on the guest list and where are they sitting? Our lives are filled with people. Sometimes they last for only a brief moment in time, sometimes for a few seasons, and sometimes forever. However, it only takes that brief moment in time for them to leave a lasting, deep impression. Who you surround yourself with dictates your course in life. How you **manage those surroundings** is a game changer. People have the capacity to add or take away, enhance and teach, challenge, love, or destroy. It's all an experience and it's what we allow.

Understand the Law of Resonance

How we feel about ourselves is what we attract. Our physical body is a vibrating system filled with thoughts and desires at a unique frequency. If we look around, the people we admire the most or resent the most are reflective of ourselves. Question number three: How do you see yourself?

You may remember this from your science classes in school. It states, "All energy resonates at a specific frequency enabling only energy of a harmonious frequency to attach to it creating your physical results, or "when two energy fields vibrating at different frequencies are brought together, the resonance of the two must meet. Either the higher will be pulled down to the lower, the lower will be raised to the higher, or they will meet somewhere in between." Surrounding ourselves with those of a higher vibration signal will ultimately raise our levels. It's quantum physics.

In laymen's terms, we are who we surround ourselves with, and those surrounding us are a reflection of our confidence level, our attitude, and our self-esteem.

The Head Table

Appreciate your partners and your loved ones.

I was devastated when my grandmother passed away with ovarian cancer. I was only twenty-one and felt cheated. I remember my aunt sobbing and mumbling, "I never told her thank you for all the things she did for me in my life." The real truth is that my grandmother knew how grateful my aunt was.

Our head table consists of the most important people in our lives. These are the people that make the biggest impression, the ones we trust, the ones we love and often the ones we also sometimes take for granted. Sometimes we get so distracted with all the other people in our lives that we forget about the ones that are closest to us or aided us in our darkest moments.

These are our mentors, our close friends and our family. They have the most influence on us, and often they take on a "thankless" position in our life. There are times in our life when we expect them to be there, we expect them to have the answers, we expect them to show up, and we always expect them to help us. And when the moment comes when they cannot be there, sometimes we turn on them. We feel hurt or betrayed by their actions often without any regard to what they may be going through or what they really meant. Often, we only think of ourselves in these situations; often we only see from our perception and don't wear their shoes.

How are you managing your emotions and actions with the people you are surrounded by?

They may not always be there.

Take some time to appreciate the greatness they have brought to your life. Take some time to remember all the wonderful things they have added. Take some time to just appreciate.

The Contemplated Guest

I remember the first time I met Rachel. She was newly hired in my company by my assistant manager while I was away on a business trip. She didn't carry the image I was looking for so I immediately judged

Practice the art of being non-judgmental or less judgmental daily.

her. She was dressed to go to a nightclub, not come to an office. Without much thought, I told my assistant manager that I was disappointed in his hiring practices and I decided that this would be a great learning opportunity for him.

A few days into her employment, I received a phone call from our quality control department stating that never had they had such a person manage and control the store that she was in with such pride and passion, work so studiously with the employees there and drive the results they were seeing. He then half jokingly asked me if I could clone her and send her to every store in North America.

When she came back, I set up a business dinner with her. At that meeting, I realized that she was one of the most genuine and caring individuals that I had ever encountered. She generated so much warmth and love with a huge appetite to succeed. I was ashamed of myself for having prejudged her. And I felt the need to deeply apologize.

Rachel later became a shining star in my company and one of my best friends in life and still, to this day, fourteen years later. I guess in the end, it was a huge learning lesson, but one for me, not my assistant manager. **How are you managing your thoughts and judgments of the people surrounding you? Are you allowing your judgments to stand in the way of a potential great relationship?**

The forces of nature sometimes bring together people in odd ways. Sometimes we run into a person, unplanned and unsuspected that changes our destiny, and in those same unplanned moments, our life changes. But we must be open to the experience and open to the person. Learn to accept those in your life and open the door for new possibilities.

If your mind starts to judge or feel any unwanted emotion, stop for a moment and ask yourself, "Why is this person in my life? What lessons can I gain? How may I serve this person? Why do I feel this way and how do I change that?" Also, decide how much weight this person holds in your life.

The Unexpected Guest

This is a story about trusting in and allowing others to help. I don't believe in accidents or coincidences. People tend to show up at the right moment.

> *One summer after losing some major key players in my business and after a break up with my boyfriend of two years, I felt as though my direction and focus were lost and my whole world was at such a dangerous low. My heart was hollow, my home was empty, my energy was depleted and it was reflecting on everything in my professional and personal existence.*

I couldn't eat, I couldn't sleep, and I couldn't concentrate on one thing for an extended period of time. I remember going home one weekend contemplating the new week I had ahead of me, desperately thinking of how I would put the broken jigsaw puzzle back together. That weekend felt like a month.

Monday morning, I crawled out of bed and somehow, in a zombie state, made it to my office to be confronted by a huge surprise. One of my dearest friends, Shelly, was standing outside my office door. She used to work with me and had been there with me through some really tough times in the past. But she had moved out of the country for three years and disappeared from my life.

Shelly was my unexpected guest. However, I was resistant at first to let her in and be there for me. I wanted to mourn and stay in my helpless state. I didn't want anyone to help me. I created a wall around myself because I considered myself strong and would work it out all on my own.

After an extended power struggle with myself, I finally gave in and let her console me through my grief once more. I was astonished at how quickly her presence helped me to fill my heart with light and laughter again and reenergized my zest and focus to rebuild my business.

Life is serendipitous. I believe and trust in that. Sometimes we have to allow others to be there for us. **How are you managing the people surrounding you that are offering you advice and guidance? Are you open to their help?**

The Assistant

Having strong mentorship in our lives is the best way to quickly make some necessary changes we may need. There was a time where my male mentors were tough, even ruthless with me, and I remember never wanting to take any of their advice. I felt a constant power struggle when they regularly told me what I needed to do, or they steam rolled right over me when I attempted to give my opinion. I wasn't responsive to that type of coaching. I could make my own decisions and would do it my own way.

That attitude didn't work well and it took me a long time to understand the issue, which closed me to future guidance. I thought I just didn't need mentorship at all, that is until I found the right mentor. That was when I was introduced to a male coach who listened to my ideas and understood my emotions, challenged my ideas in the most tactful way and helped me understand my own actions. I learned that I didn't ever have to apologize for who I was but just to find a way to recognize the best parts of me.

Finding the right guidance developed my self-esteem and helped me to love the person I am. **Managing your surroundings sometimes means understanding who the right people are for you**.

The Empty Chair

How do we invite the right people into our life and let go of the wrong people?

Time for Some Weeding and Some Cultivation ... Time for Gardening

We all experience ups and downs in life. There were plenty of times I've looked around and noticed that my employees were nonproductive, unhappy and there was almost no synergy. It was to the point where I questioned why they were still there and why was I still working with them.

These were significant learning lessons for me where I realized that I was outwardly projecting a negative, nonproductive environment and allowing others to feel the same around me. It was a reflection from how I felt deep inside.

The result of living in such an environment is that there is no open door for positive, productive behavior or one for new exciting relationships to form because that sluggish environment is clogging new growth. I had to make some uncomfortable changes within myself as with my environment.

By releasing and letting go of some of the current relationships that were not working in my life, it created room for exciting new faces. It took a ton of courage. It's much easier to bring in brand new energy than wake up a relationship that is over. It's of primary importance to recognize when a relationship is at its end though and not just an escape.

How are you managing your relationships that have ended? Are you allowing yourself to let go so that both parties can move on? Managing your surroundings by letting go of that ended relationship will open the door for exciting new adventures.

Now it's time to take out your party pen and create your list!

Think about who's in your life and how do you see them. How do they add? Who's missing? What can you do to invite those people in? And whom do you need to have more faith in? All of these people on "the list" shape our lives. Get it right!

How are you managing your surrounding relationships?

Chapter 12

SNAKES AND LADDERS

Michell

Past decisions, months or years pursuing a career or course of study only to discover you want to do something else, years of loyal service cut short by being downsized, these are just a few examples of ways we can feel stolen from—if we choose to. Stolen from by bad choices, impulse decisions, and wasted time, only to be left back at the beginning again, exhausted by the thought of having to start completely over. This perspective can be crippling. A different perspective tells a different story completely …

Almost everything we do in our lives serves us somehow. Many of our experiences and choices were required to be experienced before our next ones were even available. The children's game of snakes and ladders is a more accurate playbook for life than all of us may have thought. The object of the game is to climb to the top. You do this by rolling the dice and moving your game piece the appropriate number of spaces forward. Some spaces are where a ladder begins—a ladder that ascends multiple levels at one time and gets you far ahead. Some spaces are where a snake begins—a snake that sends you back down multiple levels to attempt to climb again.

When each of us looks at the circumstances we are surrounded by, our ability to find where we can productively put our efforts to get closer to where we want to end up is the only strategy that will help us. Staying suspended looking for the exclusive direct route will in most cases make us lose years of time. There is opportunity everywhere. Perhaps sometimes disguised as a detour and others as a more difficult fall … but it's there; you have to look for it to find it.

I am thankful for the game of snakes and ladders … you never know what you will get with the next roll of the dice. Understanding this helped me keep my power even through setbacks. Accepting that past choices and "mistakes" were necessary was a big perspective change for me. The only way I found to go from powerless to powerful was to find the lessons and be grateful for them. This was seriously not easy, but the only way to have learned what I've learned was to actually go through it—a heavy concept.

It took me a long time to get this perspective. Years, in fact. I thought that the first career I picked was going to give me everything I was looking for in life. I believed this wholehearted and completely until the day I no longer did. That was a devastating day. In fact, the next year was a devastating year. I could not get over how wrong I had been with some of my expectations. It was devastating to have spent over a decade climbing the ladder of success only to get to the top, and realize that it was leaning up against the wrong wall.

Finding my passion again took me some time. When I did, however, I realized that these new opportunities never would have been available to me if I had not accomplished what I had already in the first stage of my career. All of that work was not a waste. My ladder was not leaning up against the wrong building; it was only from the top of this building that my next ladder could begin.

Levels and Life

I now look at life as though it is lived on a series of levels.

All of us start off at the beginning. There are many ladders leading to a more successful life, just waiting to be climbed. Some of the ladders represent career accomplishment, some are for education, some are for spiritual awareness, but they all lead up, and they all present a challenge. Most of us do not make the climb successfully the first time, which means that when we fall, we fall back to the beginning. This "sucks."

I sometimes play videogames. Donkey Kong is one of the originals and still one of the best known. It is a game where players climb to each level and are challenged by mad little guys marching back and forth who are looking to take away our energy and force us back down to the beginning. Just as in the videogame, in life we have to avoid these guys.

They want to prevent anyone else from climbing higher because they were unable to successfully do it themselves. And there is always going to be someone at the top throwing bricks or barrels down at the climbers. That is because they did climb successfully to the top but they did it without ethics or honor. And the true price of their choices included the loss of almost every relationship they had. They are suspicious and controlling and they suspect we smile at them because we have to … and they are right.

Seeing my surroundings this way gives me the understanding and tolerance I need to forgive my own mistakes, and the courage and confidence I need to feed my insatiable desire to take another roll of the dice.

Believing that life is lived on these fundamental levels gives me the perspective I need to understand how lessons are served. Choosing to truly believe this is a choice. The value in the lessons is the highest commodity available for collection. My biggest mistakes have been my biggest teachers.

How do you choose to see the world around you?

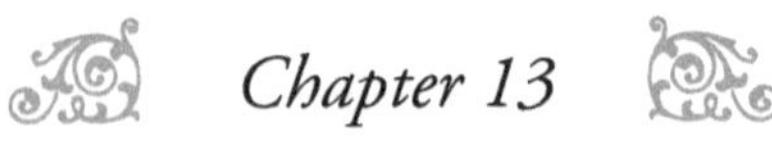

Chapter 13

NECESSARY EVILS

Julie

Plug your nose and swallow the cough syrup

How are you managing your surroundings when you are challenged by an unexpected obstacle, place, or person? How are you interpreting and integrating that into your life without getting off track? A necessary evil is something that you did not ask for, an obstacle that you did not expect, or a challenging person that disrupts your life. But, it was necessary for your future progress. The challenge is recognizing it as necessary in the present state. **How are you managing your necessary evils?**

Life happens. Things go awry, personal issues throw things out of kilter, people stand in our way for no reason we know of, and life can get complicated. Sometimes we are up at bat, ready to hit that homerun. Instead, we strike out unexpectedly. Or suddenly, someone comes along and claims our prize, takes the recognition and gets all the accolades. And in the moment of complete and utter disarray, we figuratively pull the covers over our head in embarrassment and decide to spend the rest of the year praying for remission.

Challenging people, places and things happen in our life that we didn't ask for or didn't expect.

That "Person"

Let's recognize that challenging and disruptive people exist. We feel as though they are lurking in the corner ready to attack at our most unsuspecting moment. We allow them to interrogate us, judge us, push us, disrespect us, control and compete with us, anger us, or stop us; the list is endless. We all know who these people are—for each of us. We are allowing these people to affect us this way. **How are you managing your emotions or responses to these people?**

That "Place"

It's the slump, the dumps; the place we feel defeated. There are seasons in our lives where issues have been challenging, impossible or filled with detrimental circumstances and they affect our entire world. Sometimes in the bright daylight for the world to see, that insurmountable feeling just stands there suffocating our every thought, consuming our every emotion, challenging our belief system, depleting our energy and killing our confidence. **How are you managing yourself during these times in your life?**

That Unpleasant "Thing"

This is the unfortunate set of circumstances, obstacles, losses or accidents in which we failed to plan for or got caught off guard. This is any unpleasant thing that may have changed the course of events. **How are you managing yourself when you are caught off guard?**

Life is loaded with opponents. Physical, emotional, personal—they all exist. They are all there to challenge sometimes the darkest sides of us. Some are so monumental that it seems that taking one more breath is exhausting. In my darkest moments, I was completely convinced that these "things" were more than formidable opponents. They were inescapable obstacles that I had fallen prey to and had become a punching bag in a world full of boxers. But remember, amazing victories are amazing because of the fierceness of the opponents that are overcome.

The Tutelage of Pai Mei

In the movie *Kill Bill*,, written and directed by Quentin Tarantino, there was a 1000 year-old, legendary, martial arts master of Bak Mei Kung Fu named Pai Mei who became the master for Beatrix, a white American female. He was the only known master of the fatal Five-Point Palm Exploding Heart Technique, and legend had it that he taught no one, until Beatrix wooed him over. Pai Mei was a vengeful, violent, sadistic man with a hugely inflated sense of pride. He massacred a temple of 60 monks in retribution for one that supposedly insulted him.

Pai Mei was extremely racist, and he hated everything that his student, Beatrix, symbolized. He mocked her personal belief system; he laughed at her attempts to demonstrate her abilities and consistently tried to prove to her that he is stronger, quicker, and smarter. Although, he agreed for her to be his student, he frowned upon her, mocked her abilities and did everything in his power to make her fail.

Beatrix became a master herself and from her brutal, evil time with Pai Mei and after her release, she was able to survive death's door. Being nailed into a coffin and buried alive six feet under in a grave, she used the three-inch-punch technique taught to her by Pai Mei, to punch and dig her way to safety. And in the end, she was able to thwart her lifetime enemy, Bill, with the Five-Point Palm Exploding Heart Technique and achieve justice. Pai Mei was a necessary evil.

"When the pupil is ready, the master will appear." (The master is not always what you may have imagined.)

Sometimes, we don't always have the good fortune to have a Pai Mei placed in our life on purpose. Pai Mei, although savage, was a wisdom seeker, and actively tortured Beatrix as necessary part of her training to become a master. Life is random and for most of us, Pai Mei sometimes shows up unannounced.

The Law of the Jungle

If we define the pure nature of the jungle, it's surviving in the Serengeti. In the animal kingdom, the law of the jungle is brutal. The law essentially says that you do whatever you can to survive. Power and survival are the sole virtues of the Law. It's the way in which only the strongest and cleverest people in a society stay alive or succeed; it is kill or be killed.

Though that sounds primitive, it exists in today's society. Looking back into the animal kingdom, the African lion is, without question, the king of all African predators. The Lion is also the best known, most respected and feared member of the Big Five, the five most hunted animals in South Africa. There are countless books and articles on how to outrun the lion. It's ferocious and fast. But in reality, it's not just about the race to outrun the lion itself. The lion teaches you to survive as well as to run faster than you've ever run before. The lion is the necessary evil.

Believe There's a Reason

> *You can't connect the dots looking forward; you can only connect them looking backwards. So you have to trust that the dots will somehow connect in your future. You have to trust in something—your gut, destiny, life, karma, whatever. This approach has never let me down, and it has made all the difference in my life.*
>
> —**Steve Jobs** in his commencement speech at Stanford, 2005.

Steve Jobs, the founder of Apple, in his short commencement speech at Stanford spoke about connecting the dots. He spoke about why dropping out of college led him to the founding of Apple and the development of the Macintosh computer; how being fired from Apple at the age of 30 led to his beautiful marriage; and how recovering from pancreatic cancer changed his life. Sometimes the disasters are the fuel of the future. (Steve tragically succumbed to the recurrence of his disease in 2011.)

Sometimes We Need to Lose to Win

Losing is an investment in your future. It can truly be your defining moment.

When I opened my first business in Charlotte, NC, I thought I would rule the world. I was so high on ego and pride, that I thought nothing could stop me, until day one, that is, and then day two and day three … and so on. It became an endless battle to succeed, make money, grow my business, and sell for my clients.

After twelve months of the brutality of trying to succeed and feeling no hope, I was at my wits end. I had transformed from high and mighty into a whimpering little girl. I felt as though I would have a nervous breakdown. Chipping away at myself as I had, and removing my shields, I was completely vulnerable; I thought I would break in half. I wanted to find the solution so badly that I made myself sick. I was reduced to tears almost 24/7.

After an entire year, I realized how vulnerable I was. It took all of that for me to be open to any kind of change. I was forced to look inside of myself and dig down deep. Somewhere there had to be an answer … but I kept coming up short … Until I received a phone call to shut down my business and move four states south. I was asked to work for someone again. I hoped to learn and relearn what I was missing and attempt to reopen my business there. I had nothing to lose anymore. There was no ego stopping me, I didn't try to defend the fact that I was failing miserably. I just picked up my stuff, as if in a trance, and I left.

I left with so much intent and fierce need for retaliation. The pain of failure sparked enormous energy to change my life. I drove my U-Haul with fire behind the wheel and dust trailing behind me.

The Phoenix Arises

With amazing mentorship and a humble attitude, it took only five months to reopen my business. By my efforts I found myself in the best position I could possibly be. My business skyrocketed that year and the following years were some of my most successful yet.

I realized that back in Charlotte, I was trying to reinvent the wheel. I was letting others tell me what to do, I made excuses for the people around me, and I didn't believe in myself. That ego and pride provided a great and false sense of confidence. I am eternally grateful that I failed in Charlotte. It forced me to move, meet the most powerful mentors, and change my life for the best. I am so thankful that I didn't quit in Charlotte, although I wanted to.

Charlotte was the most necessary evil, and one that I certainly never would have asked for.

Managing your emotions, reactions, and responses to your surroundings during extreme challenges can be very difficult. In periods of extreme growth are consequences of those things that throw us off-balance. The pain runs deep, or the challenge is so heightened, and we are forced to step up, make a change, grow clever, or move faster. Recognizing that the current challenges are **necessary** for your future opportunities is one of the key factors to answering question number four: **"How are you managing your surroundings?"**

Chapter 14

PICK YOUR PERSPECTIVE

Julie

Perception is reality. The key to understanding how to manage your surroundings is to understand the perspective you keep on all your daily activities and have the ability to see another point of view.

One day I was sitting in a fine dining French restaurant with a friend. I was overwhelmed by the entire experience. The food was superb, the wait staff was professional, and the place was absolutely gorgeous. We were sitting in the back corner of the restaurant and I was facing out.

What I saw was a beautiful and divine renaissance look, from paintings to wine racks, red velvet curtains and ceramic angel water fountains. The moment was so captivating that I had to ask my friend how she felt as she looked around.

She shrugged her shoulders and mumbled, "It seems just okay to me."

Then she turned around and jerked in astonishment at the view at her back. "Well," she said, "I get it now. See what I have been looking at." She gestured to the wall behind me.

I turned and looked behind me, then got up, sat in her seat and looked around. All I saw sitting in her seat was a tall brick wall in front of me and the hallway to the bathroom. There was nothing glamorous; in fact the view was nothing better than a low-end pizza joint. Since we'd entered from the back, my friend didn't notice the view until I made the remark. "Hmm," I thought to myself. What a profound moment for me.

What do you see from where you're sitting?

What if you challenged your surroundings and decided to see an opponent's point of view?

What if everything you think and see is halfway made up because of what you believe to be true?

What if the people that are accusing you of doing something are right?

In our 3-D world, there are illusive images all around us. Just as you would stare at a brainteaser and the image changes from what you originally concluded, our life and surroundings are the same in that ability to change.

Being open to another point of view and having the ability to dismantle and deprogram your own perception and your own reality of a situation can be an arduous affair. It takes years of practice. But if you make a sincere effort to consider the many points of view and the limitless possibilities that in turn lead to the limitless options and opportunities, you can begin to see the world for what it really is, and you can begin to answer question number four: **How are you handling your surroundings?**

Question Number Five:

HOW WELL DO YOU HANDLE THINGS WHEN YOU FEEL YOU AREN'T WINNING?

What you do when you feel things aren't going your way is a revealing piece in the puzzle.

Trigger-Happy

Julie and Michell

Question number five is:
"How well do you handle things when you feel you aren't winning?"

A lot of times we feel as if we are not winning because we let others get the best of us. So then it's easy to let our emotions run away with us. Ever feel as though there is a target on your back and someone knows how to push your buttons? And boy, they do it well!

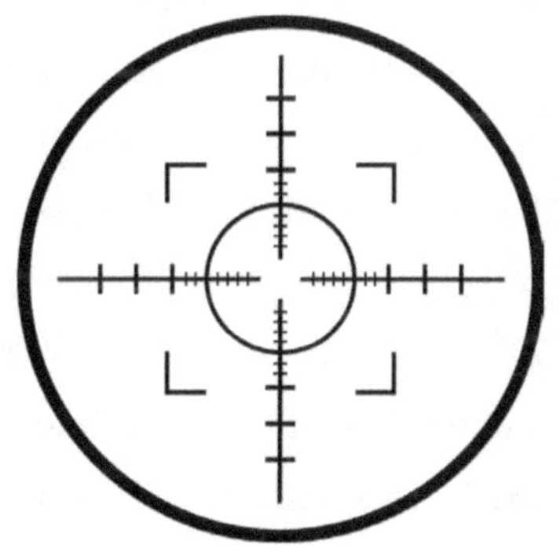

There are people that keep popping up in our lives; they have different names, different titles, and there are different settings; nevertheless they always seem to be the same formidable opponent. They always seem to be the same person. If you put those people together in one room, you would notice the same characteristics in all of them. These are the people that challenge our emotional responses. **How well do you handle yourself around these people?**

They seem to make piercing comments that prey on your insecurities, be it with a glance, a sneer, a shake of their head, or a roll of their eyes. This can destroy your emotions, shatter your ego, and shake your confidence to your core. You feel unjustly judged by these people. You feel as though their rationale is irrational and that their logic is illogical. From your perspective, you were being targeted, judged, underappreciated, underestimated and attacked.

You were in their line of fire and it's easy to become defensive as a result.

Sometimes there is a physiological response to the fear caused by the presence of this person. Fear can actually manifest when they are around and it seems as though they are feeding off of the power from this. When we encounter these people, we need to regain our power and to no longer permit their opinion to have any weight.

We thought it was because we were women, and perhaps we were right, but we were wrong in thinking that our male colleagues never had to face this same kind of career sharpshooter. To reach a high level of success in any endeavor this negative character is just a normal part of the obstacle course we are required to learn to navigate. There is no value in wasting time feeling like the targeted woman. **If our emotions are unchecked, we will allow these people to ruin our day, or worse, our career or relationships.**

There are people that love to prey on other people's insecurities. Their defense is to have a very strong offense to cover their own insecurities, therefore, they attack another's insecurities to cover their own. They attack first, fast and furious in hopes that their "opponent" will back down right away. Their adversarial approach works as long as the receiver allows it. **How well do you handle things when you feel you aren't winning?**

Most of the time they are people that, from the start, we have trouble communicating with, leading to incorrect assumptions and creating a mountain of insecurity between both parties from imagined perceptions.

Disarm Your Sniper

1. Stop reacting to their mess:
   A therapist friend told me once, "**Your opinion of me is really not any of my business.**" Remove your emotion and see a different perspective. Someone else's truth is not your truth. Someone else's problems and issues are not your problems and issues unless you make them your problems and issues. Remove their opinion because you are no longer interested.
2. Look in the mirror:
   Where are your emotions coming from and why is this person affecting you? The problem you have with this person may be what you need to fix about yourself.
   Are they there for you to learn to stand up for yourself or to control your emotions? Or are they mirror imaging what you don't like in yourself?
   In *The Road Less Traveled*, M. Scott Peck writes,

> *The problem of distinguishing what we are and what we are not responsible for in this life is one of the greatest problems of human existence ... we must possess the willingness and the capacity to suffer continual self-examination.*

3. Stop trying to fix them:
   You'll waste your life trying. There is an old French saying, "*Pas de lieu Rhône que nous*" or, "Paddle your own canoe." Handle your own affairs. Chances are, the grass needs watering under your own feet. Focus on yourself; you'll see incredible improvement.
   I often hear questions like, "How can I change my team members?" "How can I change my spouse? Mahatma Gandhi, one of the world's leaders in his ability to instill non-violence in the behavior of a nation said, "You must **be** the change you wish to see in others."
   We cannot change anyone, we can only change ourselves.
4. Stop trying to please them:
   You'll keep enabling them. You line up, they shoot you down and then you line up again. Stop lining up and change the way you are reacting. People treat us the way we teach them to. Take responsibility in the relationship. Do your work, live your life, stop steering, and trying to win something you don't need.
5. Try to understand them:
   What's going on in their life that is driving their behavior? People project out their inner fears onto others sometimes and you may be the target. Continue to treat them with respect and understand why they are acting the way they are. It's not really about you. Approaching them with an

understanding viewpoint can lesson and sometimes even alleviate the pain.

6. Understand your participation in the relationship:
   Maybe you are unintentionally carrying a machine gun ready to fire at someone else's target. The more you judge the person and the more you react negatively, the more it will fuel the fire. Acknowledge your participation. When you shift your thinking to a more positive and understanding state, others tend to shift with you.

When you feel as though you aren't winning, how are you treating others around you?

When your firing squad realizes that they have no target, they lower their guns.

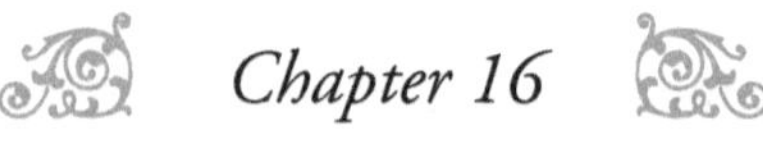

Comfortably Uncomfortable

Julie

When you feel you aren't winning, how well are you handling things? The answer to this question lies in your ability to gage your current situation. Getting it right is making some wise decisions on altering your course. Being comfortably uncomfortable means that you are not comfortable, but you are not willing to do anything about it, therefore, convincing yourself that you are OK. This is a form of denial. It's hard to understand your emotions and handle things accordingly when you convince yourself that you are winning in your environment, when deep inside, you know that you are not.

Complacency Can Lead to Burn Out

At a mid-point in my career, things in my life and work had changed. I didn't want to go to sleep at night because I didn't want to wake up and go to work in the morning. I felt stuck. I felt no motivation. Perhaps it was depression, maybe it was exhaustion, maybe it was the repetition in my life but I feeling as though I was doing the same thing over and over and over, spinning my wheels. Where are my results? Why is it that I felt like I was pouring my energy into something, expecting, hoping that eventually my law of averages would kick in?

Law of averages (LOA): "more equals more." The more you do, the law says, eventually your results will appear.

I believed that. But what if you are running faster, but you are only running in place; are you really going anywhere? If you are running in place, the LOA won't work. Is it plain and simple? Are the mechanics wrong?

Yes, it's simple … The car won't drive if the tires are flat.

Groundhog Day

Michell

I liked that movie. The concept of living the exact same day over and over again in the movie was funny … in my life, however, it was not. I couldn't pinpoint when the change occurred. I don't know whether it was because of a disappointment or a specific event; I just know that one day my life felt like *Groundhog Day.*

I was no longer energized by my work. I was at a standstill in a relationship I no longer felt connected to. I felt as though I was numbly going through the motions of this life, one that I had written like a script, and there was no end in sight, no final scene.

"How did I get here?" The question was playing on a loop inside my head. The same tasks and challenges were re-appearing over and over and over again; the same fires would burn at the offices of my business in different cities and require the same process to put them out. The sense of accomplishment I got while climbing the ladder to the top faded away once I was there. There was nothing left, I thought, I was driven to chase. The pursuit of new challenges and new puzzles to solve, the entrepreneurial challenges that I loved had faded away into the shadows of the administrative workload required to run what we had built. I looked and I only saw my shadow. The girl who got me here was gone.

I had changed. I wanted something … different; but I didn't know exactly how to transition to that yet. So my days became routine and passionless for a time. The hollowness of trading pieces of my life doing something I was no longer completely energized by was like being haunted. The impossibleness of figuring out how to change this paralyzed me.

I allowed time to pass because I had not yet come to a solution. Days upon days of performing the same tasks that I'd performed for a decade. Do you know when you feel like that? It is like there is nowhere else for you to grow by continuing in the same role, but you have no idea how to stop because it defines you? Like a pro athlete who gets injured, and doesn't know how to do anything else? This turned me inside out. My "stuckness" overwhelmed me, and I failed for a while. I failed to make a decision. I failed to figure it out.

I stayed in the game like a player riding the bench.

Every day.

For years.

I was looking for my shadow and the proud figure that used to cast it.

"How did I get here?"

The Comfort Trap

Julie

I was uncomfortable, but not willing to do anything about it.

It's hard to find the energy to handle things when you feel you aren't winning. Resistance to change is universal. This stems from fear of the unknown and enough feeling of comfort in the current situation. It's easy to convince ourselves that the current situation is fulfilling enough even if it isn't. It's easy to live in denial about one's current state of affairs and tell ourselves that everything is just fine. Most likely, we are unmotivated and uninspired by any perceived alternatives that require energy and work to make the change. This resistance involves perception in part, partly mental equipment, and partly an apparent lack of resources and support.

People generally settle into dissatisfying situations in their life because they are too reliant on the certainty of the current situation. Too much comfort in certainty can lead to what we call the "comfort trap." They feel lost and lackluster. They are either unclear of or afraid of what they want, don't know where to start, are not dissatisfied enough to make a change, or are completely unaware that there may be something better. They are comfortably uncomfortable. **When you feel you aren't winning, handling things may be a moot point because you don't feel like you are losing enough to make a change.**

How do you manage fear and resistance? How do you inspire yourself when you are comfortably uncomfortable? How do you even know that there is room for change?

Seven years into running my business, I remember being at an all-time, emotional low. After feeling as though a tidal wave came through and knocked out my office, I felt stuck.

I remember my office space. I was sharing space with another sales office that worked different hours than I did but we shared the meeting space. Each morning, the other manager would come barreling in early, swing open the door, cross his arms and just stare at me as I was talking to my reps. That was his passive-aggressive, bully way of saying, "You're taking too long and I need the meeting space." He was very disrespectful, made sexual demeaning comments to me, and was very untrustworthy. I could have easily filed a sexual harassment case against him. However, I was at such a low, that I didn't even have the energy to move in that direction. I am not sure why I tolerated his attitude, but I do remember that his presence contributed to my feelings of inadequacy when running my business.

I remember my handful of capable reps. There was no common goal, no synergy. They all had their own agenda. I was bending the rules because I felt as though I needed those leaders to keep the doors open. I was stuck in this vacuum of frustration. I didn't have the energy or the motivation to change things. My bills were getting paid, and I was getting by. I was just showing up and playing to get by, but not to improve or win.

Pain Setting In

We had a few small bathrooms inside of our office and the toilet next to my office would get backed up daily from that other manager I worked with. It was pretty disgusting. He would purposely walk to my side of the building and use that bathroom every morning.

Across from the bathroom were old storage shelves built into the walls, but all of the cheap wood was cracking and peeling and there was an eternal pile of sawdust on the floor over the coffee stained carpet that seemed to always be frayed.

I had two office doors - one out to the parking lot right next to the overflowing dumpster and one oddly narrow, makeshift doorway out to the hallway. That office door broke one evening when a disgruntled rep came in and accidentally ripped it off the hinges. So, I removed it.

I experienced the same results, day after day. The office space and my loathsome partner, the location and the ripped doors, and finally the backed up toilet started building inside of me.

I was starting to feel too much pain. It was the kind of emotional boredom and pain that was forcing me to open my eyes and make some changes.

I Was Comfortably Uncomfortable

That weekend, I fell asleep late Friday night watching a film. It wasn't a great movie but the remote control was too far away for me to change the channel. I was freezing and uncomfortable, but didn't feel like getting up because I was too tired. I fell asleep only to wake up later to a stiff neck and frozen toes.

That didn't have to happen. I convinced myself that I was comfortable enough. I settled in.

Then Came the Epiphany

It was that moment that I woke up, stiff and freezing, that I realized that I need to force some energy back into myself and start moving.

When we are stuck, the one thing that can propel us forward is to experience enough of the bad situation that we can no longer stand it, or we can have something so unbelievably desirable that we must change to have it.

For me, the pain had set in too deeply, forcing a reaction.

It was clearly time for a change. I mustered the courage to find another office space on my own, hire new productive reps, and take on another client. It took only four months from that change to see huge improvements in my business. I heard later that my past loathsome business partner went out of business.

Are you feeling the same emotional boredom every day? How are you handling things during this time period? The best way to overcome the comfort trap is to get out of your own environment.

- Find someone who has earned the life style that you want and visit them. What have they done to improve their life? With their example, what changes can you make to improve your life?
- Find someone that is not as fortunate as you. This may help you appreciate your life or give you the boost you need.
- Maybe it's time for a change! When the passion and the magic are dead, this could be a clear indicator that it's time to move on. This will take a lot of courage and time alone to find clarity again in what your heart wants.

Learning to handle things when you feel you aren't winning is a key to your success. If you wait to handle things, and if you are stuck for too long and don't make changes, changes will be made for you …

WAKE-UP CALL

Michell

Mine was brutal. Really facing what I thought about my life after a season of success was one of the toughest things I've ever done. I was proud of what I'd accomplished thus far, but I was unhappy … really unhappy. Succeeding at achieving my goals only to realize that I now wanted different goals was like driving a truck into a brick wall in sixth gear.

I was paralyzed as a result of this "crash" for a time, and stayed that way, unconscious I think, because I did not know what to do. That's when my wake-up call occurred. Wake-up calls happen when you leave yourself no other choice …

Apparently my voice had been trying to get my attention for ages, showing up occasionally like an update pop-up does on your computer, and I'd been clicking the "remind me later" button for years.

I was stuck and it had been easier to pretend that everything was fine … for a while. The truth was I was way off-track and pretending I wasn't; wasn't going to help me. I was disconnected and in search of passion in my life again. "Doing time" in the meantime was no longer an acceptable sport to play. (Taking actions that would have forced this chapter to be titled "Crime Scene" instead were equally unacceptable.) I had searched out advice from everyone around me and knew that I was simply prolonging the inevitable. I had to actually let myself hear myself and I knew I was going to be in trouble when I did.

Although it can feel "paralyzingly" overwhelming … it is progress to learn this, and progress is all that counts. The alternative is to stay stuck, and this option does not carry with it a happy ending or existence. "Stuckness" "sucks."

I'm not saying it is easy. I am not saying it is pretty. In fact, "natural disaster" is probably the closest descriptor for what it is like. But surviving the storm and coming out the other side to me was finally a more acceptable option than hiding in the eye of the storm, pretending that everything was fine … while silently screaming inside.

Terrified of what would come next, I finally did what I knew I had to do.

I listened to my voice.

It said, "Revamp your career, end your relationship, get back in shape, sell your house, and find your passion again." Pretty much change EVERYTHING that existed in my world. Everything that I had handpicked and created in the first place—change it all. I was terrified.

Instead of listening when this first happened to me, I distracted myself. I would re-arrange my office, start a new project, renovate something, landscape something or decorate something and make lots of lists.

My incessant productive, denial-oriented reaction was to constantly fix or change things around me and it took me years to see the light. Running out of things to renovate, made me realize that I needed to change things within me. I needed to renovate me inside, instead of giving my house another face lift.

It will save you time and money if you learn to listen to your inner voice.

Do not get distracted or busy or too tired to do this. I spent an additional five years staying stuck because I changed the channel on the voice that frightened me with its words.

Your voice, like mine, might be a little gun shy to speak up at first. It is highly aware of the fact that it has been ignored for years. It may have very little to say at the beginning and you will have to build its confidence.

Finding out what my voice had to say took acceptance and patience and encouragement and trust and time. Building a relationship with your voice is one of the most important relationships you need to build. My voice needed me to prove that I trusted it before it trusted me.

Journaling helped. Talking out loud to myself helped. **For the most part talking to others did not! Surprise!**

When I say I was shocked to hear what my voice had to say, I mean it literally knocked me off my feet. I was confounded at how I could have honestly created a life where virtually everything I had created was wrong … and I did it all by choice.

I had spent so much time with my blinders on that I forgot about checking in with myself to see if I was okay. I was nowhere close to okay.

So, how do you find your voice?

Get some time completely alone somewhere quiet and relaxing—even if it's only for ten minutes.

Sit still and just exist for a minute. Try your best to just sit without engaging your mind to work on anything … just sit.

Then ask yourself a few questions:

- How are you?
- What is good and what is not good?
- What do you want to do about that?

These pure and simple questions carry the answers that tell us the truth.

I regularly repeat this exercise. It only takes two to three minutes of my time to do it, but a check-in to hear confirmation that I am on the right track is all the energy I need to keep going. Now the voice is like a cheerleader because she knows I'm listening and she's excited.

I found that talking with others about this process did not help. My timid little voice, (because of the fabulous ignore job I'd done on it all these years), did not need any other judgment placed upon it from others. I realized that my voice was not attempting to get anyone else's attention **but my own.**

LISTEN to your voice.

Next I found the right mentors.

Spending time with the right people is a bigger deal than most of us realize. A trusted friend, a neighbor or colleague, a teacher or relative—advisors come in many forms. It is any other voice we choose to listen to with intent and allow to influence our own voice directionally.

I do not mean to negate the advice that says listening to others about the process does not help. It is important not to let your voice be drowned out by others. Those other voices are only to help guide, not demand, or change.

Finding the right advisors gives us the kind of confirmation we need to make the changes we want to make. They keep us accountable and encourage us in the right ways.

The right advisors also know that our own voices hold more wisdom than theirs do, so they encourage us to trust ourselves first.

I have had few great mentors in my life. The times that I have felt the strongest was usually because of the guidance of one of these mentors who I trusted. I believe that having the right mentors around you is required for successful growth. They are like stars guiding the journey … Always available and always with answers but are only useful if you look up at them.

How do you find the right advisors? There are two distinct questions we need to ask when we look for an advisor:

1. **Who can teach me what I need to know?**
2. **Who will help me feel the way I need to feel?**

By answering these questions we generally find the advisors we are looking for. Some people serve as mentors in certain areas of life but not in others. This is normal. Filtering through advice can be tough;

answering the above two questions is easy. Considering the advisor before the advice is the best place to start.

Approaching a mentor to ask for coaching can be intimidating. The only way to discover if they are available for you as a mentor is to ask them. Generally it is simplest to be brief and up front. For example:

Gary, I am working on a few things that I could really use some feedback on. I don't know what your availability is or commitments are but I would love it if I could book some time to get some advice from you. What do you think?

This will either lead to some time getting booked, or a response declining. Either way you know if this mentor is an option, and you repeat this process until you find one.

Some tips when communicating with a mentor:

- Be prepared. When you meet with your mentor have specific questions ready and a way to record the information you receive.
- Be respectful of the time you have together and focus on remaining on task. Most of the time you are with your mentor, they should be doing the talking. You learn nothing when your own lips are moving and if you are looking for an outlet—this is not a mentor. Your mentor will be less inclined to continue to work with you if they feel you are trying to display your own knowledge rather than acquire theirs.

"Stuckness" "sucks." The challenge with stuckness is that in order to go forward you have to go backwards first. We resist going backwards so we hang onto where we are which keeps us stuck. We press "snooze" and pretend for a while longer.

Like a car that is stuck on a hill, wheels spinning, getting nowhere except dirty, we have to back up in order to get a run at the hill that's been stopping us.

Learning to stay cool and strategic when things go wrong is necessary. We will all go through seasons of winning and seasons without winning—all of us. Handling things as best you can, staying positive and trying again is the only road back to glory.

My Wake-Up Call saved my life. Well, first it actually devastated my life, because it forced me to be honest. But it also forced me to become aware, and becoming aware was required to make changes. Things don't change by themselves.

How well do you handle things when you feel you aren't winning?

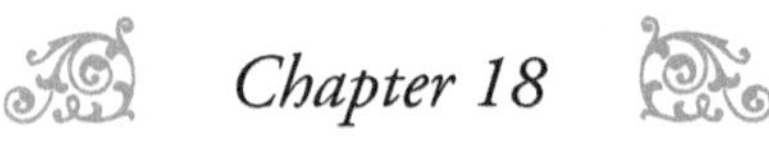

Attitude Anonymous

Michell

I *want to get my hopes up …*

When I wasn't winning as a teenager, I used to throw myself off the attitude cliff. I'd completely embrace "the victim mentality," misery and sadness, and isolate myself in feelings of incapability and exhaustion. As an adult I wanted to change this way of reacting.

How we all choose to handle things when we feel we aren't winning is mostly a matter of mindset … when I hadn't yet developed a strong positive mindset, hearing that I needed to, just pissed me off more.

I needed all the help I could get. Deciding to work on my mindset every day felt like I was in a rehab program, and I suppose that I truly was. I named it *Attitude Anonymous*, built a website and joined as the first member. It made me feel more committed and official somehow.

The reality was that I had lost my attitude … again! Actually admitting that I may have to try to have a better attitude in my twenties was the single largest step forward I had ever taken at that point in my life. The discomfort that came with accepting I was really going to have to work on my attitude—was almost overwhelming. I was my biggest obstacle and I was determined to reprogram myself. The exorcism I did in my twenties worked … until my life was different over a decade later. And the challenge then was one of a different kind.

After a season of success in my life, I once again was faced with a struggle to feel happy and satisfied, as some of the most important pieces of my life were broken. There were no angry personalities to cast out, but a tired, exhausted girl who had done her best, and succeeded, but was unfulfilled. I needed to find the strength to keep going. Failure had never been an option I could accept. The place where I had to begin was with the annoying lesson I so prolifically teach when I'm motivated … I had to get my attitude back and start to make choices with purpose.

A great coach once told me, "The greatest stumbling block to massive success is *some* success."

I am grateful for this lesson, from this particular coach. It was one of the reasons my stuckness made sense to me … and equally pissed me off. I had done it … what was required … I had accomplished what was asked and had succeeded. There is pride in that, and some comfort. Actually, a lot of comfort ... so much comfort that the money I saved and was still making from those years of dedicated work to build a business kept supporting my lifestyle for years. Discomfort is what made me work so hard in the beginning and unless I could find either the discomfort again or a new passion to chase—the next level would never be climbed by this player.

I found a reason. More appropriately, I *felt* a reason … in my soul. For every woman who has ever felt the way I felt. For every brave entrepreneur who invests everything … For every dreamer who dares to chase it, for every girl who has ever wanted some advice from someone who's been there … for perhaps the one person I might reach. I wanted to teach, to assist and to serve, and to expose my own struggles so that others might find strength—"You are not in this alone, and we are meant to win."

I wanted honor back as the primary driver in my life, and I was daunted by the road—the task—but I sought that driver anyway. The new ladder I was working to climb was one that no one I knew had ever navigated, and I, for the first time in my life, out of the destruction and the ashes, had found my "calling." I was no longer going to hide in the wings unsure; I was going to fight through to succeed at this new endeavor.

There were very specific things that helped me stay "in the zone," to be able to follow my dream. These things saved my life. Their power is of a kind that I admire … this truly allows you influence, and influence is all you need.

Step 1: Edit your Surroundings

Everything we see and experience has influence on us. Whether we register it at the time or not, we feel a certain way about the things that live in our worlds around us. When I got out of a relationship that did not work I discovered that certain things in my house triggered me to feel badly. Feelings of anger, disappointment or failure showed up when I saw certain objects in my home.

I removed them. I was amazed at how the feeling of my house changed when everything inside provided me with positive feelings.

Every object carries with it a meaning—that meaning is either positive or negative.

Remove any objects that "lower" you. Get rid of any mementos, books, dishes, gifts, music, movies, photos, clothing, and jewelry—**anything** that reminds you of something (or someone) that makes you feel less.

Fill your environments (home and work) with things that you love. Things that pay you when you look at them; they make you feel **warm**, safe, happy, secure; they make you smile or laugh, remind you of great friends, good times and past accomplishments.

Step 2: Talk to Yourself

There is a reason for the commonly spoken term "waking up on the wrong side of the bed." Sometimes we all wake up with the wrong mindset, or in a really foul mood. I've learned to set up my morning the night before.

For me waking up is just like turning on my computer. My desktop has to wake up. All of the programs that are currently saved to my desktop do a quick wake up run-through as soon as I do. I open my eyes, look at the clock and think about my life, my finances, my week, my day, my shopping list, my relationship (or lack of one) my family, my work responsibilities, my health, my body, my wardrobe, my to-do list, my stresses, my work-out schedule … And then I'm awake for 30 seconds … As a result, this sometimes meant that my days would begin in a stressed out place before I was even awake for one minute.

I would then have to go about the routine of attempting to get in a good mood, or just stay in a bad one. This was not worth it. I had to learn to conquer this because my commitment to hitting my goals was complete. I learned a way to stop myself from going through this process—and it is by talking to yourself with bedside messages.

Emotions are smart, and they are sneaky. "Worry" has learned that when I am conscious, she doesn't stand much of a chance – so she waits until I am unconscious, and she attacks. The second my eyes open, in the middle of the night, she's wide awake and waiting to take over my mind. Midnight messages have taught me how to beat her too.

During the most challenging period of my young adult life I began this practice as a survival mechanism. I knew I needed to stay positive to have a chance at making it through my current circumstances and believing I was "done for" was certain failure—this I did not—could not—accept. So—I wrote messages to myself … from myself … to see the second that I woke up.

I would say my evening prayers (I was pulling out all the stops for help—I hadn't prayed since I was 15) and place my "morning card" or my "midnight message" beside my clock—so that I would see it immediately when I woke up.

My first morning cards said things like "just breathe" and "I believe in you"; my midnight messages were more assertive, like "Stop it, we already decided things will be fine" and "Don't go there …" There were about 10 different messages I needed myself to hear. What would happen is that I would wake up and look at the clock, see the message and stop for a second. My mind was no longer running its default desktop start up program … I had learned to stop it.

Words of caution here … the first time you do this, you might wake up, read the message and think "whatever." The same with the second day and perhaps even the third, but by the fourth or fifth day you will start to allow yourself to listen to hear yourself; our resistance even to ourselves is pretty tough to break through at times.

Because of this experience I became aware of the need to learn how to accept compliments from others too. So many of us do get them, but reject them, so we don't get them anymore, and that upsets us…. (No wonder men don't understand us … we are a crazy species.)

The power that these morning messages will give you will shock you. Use a sticky note, a recipe card, any scrap of paper, whatever floats your boat. But the week you begin to wake up to your morning messages, the results after a few days will excite you. We have control; we always have … now it is time to use it.

Step 3: Sole Possession of the Remote Control

You are what you eat … listen to … and let in.

You are exactly who you choose to be. So choose.

I have seen the movie *Rudy* over 100 times. Whenever I want encouragement I pick one of my best weapons … I watch *Invincible*, or *A Knight's Tale*, *Patch Adams*, or *Remember the Titans. U571*, *Legally Blonde*, *The Replacements*, *Mystery Alaska*, *Coach Carter*, *Erin Brockovich*, *Working Girl*, *G I Jane*, *Miracle*, *Secretariat*, *Braveheart*, *Apollo 13*, *Gladiator* or *8 Mile* … I watch every underdog success story I can find.

I listen to Pink like a religion. It seems that when I won't listen to anyone else, I'll listen to her. To me, she's real, and honest and vulnerable and tough. She's been with me through my whole crazy journey, every single day … for years. She keeps the fighter in me alive and well.

The people I keep close to me are all positive souls. I've taken my own advice. They too believe in the power of dreams.

No one, and I mean no one, who speaks "discouragement" is permitted to stay in my broadcast range … it is a language I choose not to learn, and I am not interested in any interpreter.

All of us choose. We feed ourselves what we want to. I call it the law of consumption: What we consume nourishes us. Whether we believe this or not is irrelevant … the law is still the law.

Step 4: Always Carry Insurance

I can be negative like a champ. I do not spend a lot of time unhappy, but it seems when I do, I go all out. This unhappy version of me is a tough girl to negotiate with. BUT … I have learned a trick that gets through to her.

I carry insurance.

I carry insurance that I will not stay discouraged … insurance against this state of mind.

A long time ago during a really happy time in my life I wrote a message to myself on a sticky note. It was a private pat on the back that I felt compelled to write down. I put this in my wallet and forgot about it.

Several years later I had a meltdown. I was struggling and sad, unhappy with work and consumed with surviving the wasteland that remained after the breakup of a long relationship. I fell apart.

I had support from friends and family but in that state of mind my resistance was strong. I was completely committed to my new, hopeless me.

On yet another sad day, rich with actual physical, broken hearted pain, I accidently came across the message. I read it. Then dismissed it as another example of how foolish I was and how "I clearly had no idea what I was talking about back then."

But it infected me.

I went back to it. I read it again.

I was not alone.

I had a very strong voice with me—one that believed in me, one that I trusted.

I knew I meant what I wrote.

That moment is when hope showed up.

That moment is when my strength started to come back.

I read that message over and over.

I found this girl again because of that message.

I'm the only one who can get through to me, and I did.

There is a famous story called *The Devil's Yard Sale* where the tools of the devil are being sold and the most expensive tool is *discouragement*. He explains that it is because this tool is the most powerful and effective one of all. Once a hint of discouragement creeps into someone they are certain to fail. Well, my best tool to fight discouragement is this message. It is the honest and pure voice of belief. It is my wisest voice. Hope arrives every time. With hope I feel unstoppable.

I call these messages insurance cards. These insurance cards are the best investment I've ever made. They are my best kept secret.

Step 5: Have a Recognition Ritual

Recognition is a powerful thing. Getting noticed for a job well done, a simple "thank you," the tiniest things are sometimes the most important to us.

A study was done by The Society of HR Management in the year 2000; it stated that 79 percent of all people who resigned during that year and who took part in this study in America did so because of a "lack of recognition or appreciation." This tells us a few but important things:

1. We mostly stink at recognizing each others' efforts.

2. Leaving a job only to take a new one at a place that the other 79 percent of the people who quit did so for the same reason, isn't going to fix the issue.
3. Getting recognition should not be dependent on coming from others; it should come first from us.

A recognition ritual is something that serves as a reminder that we are proud of ourselves. There are many ways to do this:

Have a wall of fame somewhere in your life.

Future accomplishments are fueled by victories of the past and your faith in your own ability to win again. Many successes are followed by periods of struggle. It is important to remember that when you have won in the past it was because of your strengths; that will enable you to find those strengths to win with again.

Treat yourself.

Ordering something small, as a "way to go" that will be delivered in the future like a subscription to a magazine that you love (for me it's the hockey news magazine) pays you over and over again. Every time it arrives you get a little lift as the intention behind the ordering of it was to remind you that "you've done good kid." Now, when I take a break to read my magazines—I feel good the whole time. When I see these same magazines ANYWHERE—I am reminded that I'm taking good care of myself.

Plan a reward.

Half the fun of setting goals is celebrating the progress you make towards accomplishing them. An afternoon at the spa, a dinner with great friends, a concert or a trip, all pay you dividends. (Purchasing something for your office or home that you've been wanting does the same thing.) The intention behind each of these is to thank yourself for your efforts, and as a result of this intention—the ticket stub you keep or the photo at the concert will continue to thank you each time you see them.

Take time to say thank you.

We run around to buy gifts of appreciation for others when we don't really have the time, we need to take the time to say "thank you" to ourselves for our efforts too even when we "don't have the time." Take a class, take a walk, or take an afternoon … To just … Sit.

Turn the volume down on everything else in your life and allow yourself to hear the words "thank you." It's exactly like coming up for air.

Step 6: Look for Others

They are closer than you think—people who believe in possibility, people who believe in hope. The more we recognize this in each other the easier it is to stay on track ourselves. Sometimes all you need is one other person to help you find your strength again. One person helped me find mine …

The effort that gets put in at this stage is defining. What you want in your life is possible if you are willing to fight to get it. You are purely and truly fighting for your life, and you are not alone.

Honestly being able to answer question number five: "How well do you handle things when you feel you aren't winning?" is in some ways the most vulnerable truth to face. In many cases we react badly when we feel we aren't winning and this behavior can be hard to admit … all the more reason to change this going forward, to learn how to make different choices. It's like standing at a cross roads in your life. But our individual potential and capability to comeback from struggle is one of the strongest forces that lie inside all of us. How would you like to feel you handle things when you aren't winning?

How would you like to start winning again?

Question Number Six:

WOULD YOU BET ON YOURSELF TO WIN?

The honesty of this answer is inescapable.
Bet on yourself to win.

GLADIATOR

Julie

**Question number six is:
"Would you bet on yourself to win?"**

Betting on yourself to win will at some point in your life inevitably require a great comeback. No one keeps winning without experiencing the defeat. When faced with the greatest of defeats, the massive courage it takes to make some painful decisions and remember and trust in who you are can be the most daunting of tasks. This is the time to seek the great gladiator within.

My name is Maximus Decimus Meridius, Commander of the Armies of the North, General of the Felix Legions, loyal servant to the true emperor, Marcus Aurelius. Father to a murdered son, husband to a murdered wife. And I will have my vengeance, in this life or the next.

—Maximus, from the movie, *Gladiator,* written by David Franzoni, John Logan, and William Nicholson and directed by Ridley Scott.

"Maximus was a general who became a slave, a slave who became a gladiator, a gladiator who defied an emperor. A hero will rise."

—Maximus: *What we do in life echoes in eternity.*

Gladiator is one of my favorite movies. Not only because he avenges his injustice, but because it signifies the old adage, "You can't keep a good man (or woman) down."

Maximus was a great general of the Roman army. He led his men into battle and won great victories. He was betrayed by Commodus, son of the emperor Marcus Aurelius, when Commodus realized that Marcus wanted to name Maximus the heir to the throne, rather than his own son. Commodus, in a fit of jealousy, kills his father and sends Maximus off to his death. Maximus escapes and is captured by slave traders, sold, and sent to gladiator school where he becomes an unknown gladiator. He is sent to fight in the Roman coliseum and leads his fellow gladiators to many victories against much more powerful forces. In the end, he rises again as a great leader, defeats Commodus, and leads his team to victory as he wins over the Coliseum spectators and all of Rome.

Maximus proved that by having strength of the heart and doing the right thing, being courageous, loving, and with a ton of human determination, you can rise again.

He taught his army to stick together. He fought for what was right. He proved that once a great leader, always a great leader, regardless of title.

I often felt like Maximus when he was betrayed and then sold into slavery. It's not that I had an emperor out to destroy or betray me. But somewhere, lost in the middle, I realized that I took a giant leap off the cliff and landed somewhere unknown. I was defeated, beat up, lost and without direction. After great shifts with clients, a strategy of guesswork, the usual politics, and some questionable decisions, my large organization of managers and offices broke in half and broke in half again.

I questioned my own leadership. The clients that I trusted were gone. I didn't have another person to consult with that I trusted, I felt betrayed by my own goals, and I lost the courage to fight at the time. I could have been sold into slavery and wouldn't have known the difference. I was a slave in my own world.

The movie *Gladiator* did it for me. Sometimes we lose so that we can win again.

Our strength is defined in times of challenge. In order to succeed again a new battle has to be fought. The battle the second time, though, seems way easier than the first. The resources we all have within us are infinite and once their awakened, it's unstoppable. Creating greatness in our lives once takes incredible courage, commitment, work ethic, ambition and resilience. Creating it over and over again requires all the magic ingredients learned the first time. Just reapply. We know this because we've done it before. If we only define ourselves by our past successes and what we once accomplished, it can handicap us in future endeavors. Rather, we must remember the strength and endurance that succeeding required the first time, and find that same power inside ourselves again.

I bet on myself to win. I looked deep within and remembered what got me there the first time around. **Betting on yourself to win sometimes requires a great comeback.** Remembering who you are and what you've overcome in the past fuels that comeback.

We succeed because we have it in us. **The champion lies within…**

Greatness reappears in most of our lives as long as our heart remains involved.

Nothing can beat the heart of a champion. Bet on yourself to win.

Become the Gladiator, visit us at www.JulieandMichell.com

Chapter 20

PERSONAL MAGIC

Julie

Feeling confident about who you are requires inner strength, confidence, and a resolute belief that you can create positive outcomes in your life. Positive things happen to positive people. The stakes are higher and the odds are in your favor when you are following what your heart intended for you to do. Finding your own personal magic is connecting to your inner self. What is your personal magic? Betting on yourself to win does not mean that someone else is losing. Betting on yourself to win means that you are putting yourself in the best possible outcome for the best possible things to happen to you.

Do you believe in miracles?

Do you kindle a passion for something more in life? Is your heart beckoning you for something?

Finding your personal magic is about embracing the incredible force you were meant to be.

We all have callings and cravings. We are all born with amazing gifts and natural talents and it is up to us to utilize them in the most positive light, to share with the rest of the world. What is yours? Where is your personal magic? What is it? What is easy for you to do?

Are you courageous? Do you have a great sense of humor? Do you have an amazing ability to remember names and locations? Are you a talented painter or writer? Do you connect with animals? Are you charismatic? Are you a master chef naturally? Do you have an affinity for plants? Are you proficient in many languages? Do you have the ability to make others feel great about whom they are? Are you a healer? Do you have a way with people? Can you sculpt? Can you play or strum an instrument without lessons? Are you a shining athlete? Do you have a knack for technical devices? Are you skillful at interior design? Are you a graceful dancer? Are you a problem solver that people tend to gravitate towards? Do you excel in Math? Do you have a beautiful voice? Can you give an amazing presentation? The list goes on and on.

Most of these things can be recognized when you were a child. What were you drawn to? What were you naturally great at? Remember? You are made up of special gifts uniquely wrapped for you.

Unwrap your gift … relish in who you are.

The world is filled with talented people; experts and you are one of them. Find your personal magic and share it with the world.

Start by asking others who you trust what they think you are great at. Not good at, but *great* at. Just as plants and flowers blossom best under the right conditions and environments, so do our talents and gifts. Surround yourself with those who will support your gifts. Then, start creating your miracles.

You have at your fingertips the map of your destiny. **Bet on yourself to win. Put yourself in the position to win.**

"BUT OF COURSE!"

"But of course!" is my favorite saying.

This is a feeling of having resolute confidence in yourself and the world around you. But of course you do! You get the front row parking spot at the mall. Your luggage is first to come off the conveyor belt. Everyone is acknowledging your work and recognizing your efforts. Life seems effortless. But of course! But of course that happened to you. Expect it. Expect that the right people show up at the right time. Expect that the challenge you are facing is the key to unlocking a huge opportunity. Trust in yourself. **Bet on yourself to win.**

Instead of conjecturing that all the terrible, unhappy, uneventful, or unfortunate things will always happen to you, and instead of accepting the negative "but of course" attitude about them all, why not get out your helmet and brace for it, yet expect the best? Unfortunate things will happen to all of us from time to time. We discussed that in Chapter 13, *Necessary Evils* …

What if you believed that good luck was on your side all the time? What if you believed that you created that good luck? What if you expected that good things will happen to you, that there are good, trusting people in the world, and you are deserving of all the good things in life? What if you believed you can win?

The answer is, you can. And it is simple. **Bet on yourself to win.** Believe that you deserve it.

Use your personal magic ...

The very next positive thing that happens to you, say out loud "**But Of Course!!!**"

Keep doing it.

By identifying your own personal magic you give yourself the exact reasons with evidence as to why you are the best bet to win. Finding your personal magic gives you the permission you need to do what's required next.

Comfortably Vulnerable

Julie

Question number six is:
"Would you bet on yourself to win?"

Betting on yourself to win requires a confident self, giving yourself permission to make mistakes. This means giving yourself permission to be vulnerable. It also means that you can be vulnerable and safe at the same time - comfortably vulnerable.

I had a serious lesson in becoming comfortably vulnerable. There was a time when I felt as though when someone was advising me to do something different than what I originally planned, I always thought they were wrong. I pretended to listen and then I would try to tell them what was wrong with the things I did, because I had to be right about what was wrong before anyone else told me! I had to stay in control. I was betraying myself. I would say things like,

- "I know that I am responsible for part of this."
- "I know that I wasn't listening during the training call."
- "I know that I should have coached that person differently."

I somehow always had the words, "I know" in all of my answers and statements.

One of my mentors told me once, "You have to stop saying, *I know*." My answer? "I know." Of course I knew! I knew everything! I was always right. I always had to be right about what I was doing wrong so that no one else could tell me, therefore making myself right again. Hmmm …

Until the day I was terribly wrong. It wasn't days or weeks or even months. It was years of realization and awakening; years of paying attention to a class, or an analogy, or a story, or a failed attempt at something, before I realized that my perspective could possibly be wrong and to respect the fact that everyone has something to contribute.

I observed a conversation amongst two ladies one day while waiting at the valet for my car. Both of them were battling to see who could tell a better story. When the first would brag about her daughter, the second one would talk over her and louder about what her own daughter did.

As I observed this painful conversation, I started to feel the blood rise in my face and the shame in my chest.

I was that lady. I did the same thing. How embarrassing!

From that moment on and for the next year, I started dissecting everything I said and did, all my reactions and perspectives. I was very uncomfortable for a very long time. I started apologizing to the people around me for my behavior. I was vulnerable, and I wasn't comfortable.

I had to unmask my armor. I had to shed my pride. I had to put my head down and ask for help. I had to let the world know that I am a sensitive person with a ton of flaws and admit to myself that I am not always right. In fact, whatever I was doing was not right at all. It was time to listen. When I learned to trust myself again, and trust my reactions and responses, my emotions, and my decisions is when I learned to be comfortably vulnerable.

Do you trust yourself and your emotions? Do you trust the person you are? Are you honest with yourself? **The right answers to these increase the odds when betting on yourself to win.**

Sometimes the hardest thing to do is to be vulnerable. Vulnerable is defined by *dictionary.com* as: *capable of or susceptible to being wounded or hurt, open to moral attack, criticism, and temptation.*

Why Be Vulnerable?

Before we answer that question, let's discuss why we avoid being vulnerable. Avoiding vulnerability is basic self-survival in times of doubt when entering unknown territory, or from past pain, doubts and fears that have rematerialized. Lack of trust in self and others haunts us, and lack of forgiveness and inability to release injustices create barriers. Unwillingness to change, the need to remain in a safe comfort zone, or insecurity about displaying a less powerful side (for fear of being judged or rejected), are all reasons that we avoid vulnerability.

Fear of being taken advantage of is the biggest. These all hold us back from displaying our true identity and freeing ourselves from masks and insecurities. We all need a reminder sometimes of the strength that lies within each of us and the amazing freedom in allowing ourselves to be comfortably vulnerable.

Warning: Being vulnerable is not for every situation. For example, in times of impending danger or feeling trapped in an unhealthy situation, in times of trauma when you are not yet available to heal, or in business negotiations, these are not times to show your most vulnerable, sensitive side. Also, being vulnerable in a relationship where we lose touch with who we are is not healthy and is certainly not balanced. These times require a more guarded state. Lastly, toxic people can and will take advantage of vulnerability.

Should We Risk It?

- Being vulnerable first allows others to be okay with being vulnerable too.
- It allows us to let others take the lead, giving us more time for ourselves.
- It enables us to say no.
- Vulnerability builds credibility and trust.
- It allows us to say "I'm sorry" without having to defend and be right every time.
- It introduces us to new people and social circumstances, releases blockages, and opens our minds to new beliefs that may trump our old ones.
- It improves our relationships.

- It allows others around us to understand and feel better about who they are. **We all love a good failure**—mostly when it belongs to someone else. Probably because it reminds us we are not alone, and most importantly, frees our soul and well being.

Accepting us for who we are, magical and imperfect all at the same time is a tremendous accomplishment. Being open to altering our behavior patterns and beliefs eliminates bad habits.

It's not okay, though, to accept our faults and use them as an excuse for undesirable behavior.

Ask yourself these questions:

- Are you ever unable to express your emotions?
- Are you sometimes unable to let go of or forgive a past injustice?
- Do you feel overprotective of your personal space?
- Are you ever unable to cry or let others see you cry?
- Do you often hide your true feelings or never let your guard down?
- Do you feel as though you never want to love again?
- Do you sometimes have a hard time trusting others?
- Do you shy away from meeting others for fear of rejection?
- Do you often feel as though you are being judged?
- Do you feel as though some people are trying to take advantage of you?

If you answered *yes* to several of the questions above, then chances are, like most of us, you've developed some heavy armor to protect your insecurities.

How do you open up and become comfortably vulnerable and accept yourself?

Start with some of these steps and practice diligently. Once you find positive results, your confidence will resume and then soar.

- Be open to receiving. The walls you've built to protect you are also keeping positive influences out.
- Say thank you when someone compliments you rather than brushing it off. Allow yourself to let in positive re-enforcement and permit others to feel the reward of giving you this gift as well.
- Accept feedback without becoming defensive. This will be difficult at first.
- Start by expressing past experiences without blame or judgment. Allow yourself to be hurt.
- Forgive yourself and be okay with your mistakes. Why does forgiveness even exist, if not to give us permission to make mistakes in the first place?
- Tune into others, feel their feelings and emotions and listen, without feeling the need to give advice.
- Tell someone you are sorry if you are out of line; you don't always have to be right.
- Take a risk, and then another one, and then another one.
- Try someone else's ideas; other people are smart and creative too.
- Push yourself to try something new. Break comfort zones. Say hello to a stranger.
- Don't jump to conclusions about other people's motives; their intent is not always what you think it is.

- Don't be embarrassed to mourn. There are no rules to mourning.
- Be open to a change.

Understand your magic, the magic that lies within. You are a powerful person with unique skills and talents. Being vulnerable is being comfortable with whom you are. Welcome to the evolution of vulnerability.

Would you bet on yourself to win? If you can learn to become comfortably vulnerable then the answer becomes "yes." You don't feel the need to always be right, you are okay with learning and simply lean back on the purity of your intentions. You trust that the surroundings you have chosen will only propel you to succeed, and you know that you have the energy and effort to deliver the results you are after.

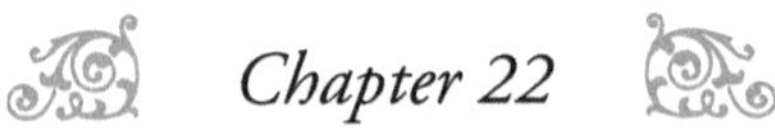

Chapter 22

Get your Swagger On!

Julie

I had to learn that there is no time to NOT be bold.

Your brain! It's time now to get in the "zone"! Getting in the "zone" will inevitably lead you down the right path. Getting in the zone is scientifically known as a heightened state of consciousness. It's called training your brain to perform. The zone or "flow state" is a universal phenomenon. It is that magical place where everything you know is automatic and exceptional. It's like your fingers autonomously playing a piano tune without you thinking about the next chord.

Have you ever been doing something so intensely that time seems to just disappear? You are so deeply focused and determined at the task at hand, that when you finally look at a clock you can't believe how much time has passed by?

You can have a successful day, every day. If you can get in the zone, you can bet on yourself to win.

Finding this magical place doesn't have to refer to athletic performance. But getting there and staying there, just as with an athlete, can be the huge dilemma. Sometimes, our brains and bodies just don't want to start moving. Or, the opposite—just as bad—is diversion activity: doing too much to avoid what really should be getting done.

I, in the past, have tended to overestimate my ability to get something done and underestimate my time being able to do it. Too busy doing everything all at once and getting nothing finished seemed to be my everyday life. The more I wouldn't get done, the more anxiety and pressure started building up. The more anxiety, the worse my mindset became and the more cluttered my life became. The more clutter, the more anxiety. It was an endless cycle.

For years, I thought I worked better in chaotic situations. Until the day I began to resent that chaos, which accompanied everything I was doing.

Realize Your Force

The term inertia means "an object at rest stays at rest and an object in motion remains in motion." But how do we generate that motion?

You can learn to force yourself to get focused and get focused quickly.

You can slow your active brain waves to concentrate on the task at hand and learn tunnel vision.

The first steps:

1. Do Something. Anything! You've heard that the key to healing writers block is to just start writing. Don't think about it, just do it. If the dishes are piled high, just pick up a dish and start cleaning. If you are procrastinating about making that phone call, just dial the numbers, close your eyes, and don't think. If you can't motivate yourself to get to the gym, just get up and put on your tennis shoes. You may be surprised at the subconscious reaction. Next thing you know, you are there and on the treadmill.
2. Turn off all distractions. Close your door, turn off your cell phone, put the kids to bed, turn off the TV, feed the hungry animals, turn the dryer buzz to silent.
3. Be your biggest fan. Tell yourself that you are great. You can do this, you have the knowledge, and you love yourself.
4. Put on your blinders. When horses are racing, they are giving blinders to block out their peripheral vision. It keeps them from distraction or being startled. Their only focus is on their forward-facing goal or vision.
5. We are all filled with infinite wisdom. Tapping into it and trusting it is the key to a healthier, smoother life. You probably do it every day at some point and don't even realize it.

The Eye of the Tiger

Michell

You know when you've got it. That unwavering, convicted knowing that things are about to get crazy in a good way. That sly sideways smile playing quietly on your face to accompany the twinkle in your eye with style; the pure confidence that has been bred through preparation and results, and the amount of work that has gone into this state of being, and as such, it is unshakable. There is the power of the eye.

Learning certain truths about yourself, self respecting truths that make you proud of who you are and give you total clarity on what you are planning next; this is where the eye comes from. You know when you own this feeling, you do it with class. Life is waiting for you to decide to own it all the time … it's time to get your swagger on.

Fall in love with the future….

Bet on yourself to win …

OUR BEGINNINGS

How Our Journey Began

Chapter 23

Imagination Playground

Michell

Growing Up

I remember summer afternoons, lying in the grass, looking up at the clouds … dreaming. The hazy sunsets painted landscapes in the sky we'd get lost in. Wild adventures we had brandishing sticks, running in the moonlight, chasing fireflies. Camping in the back yard after a game of capture the flag, roasting hotdogs and eating s'mores—the perfection of those memories is a different kind of peaceful. Indoor tents made from blankets on rainy afternoons, the smell of library books with their crinkly covers and flashlights to chase away the shadows reminds of a time when the whole world made sense. Puddle jumping was an official sport and discovery intoxicated our worlds.

All we had were our plans, and such perfect contentment with the possibility of them all....

Playing make believe is something that we are really good at, and genuinely love to do. In our early years playing make believe was all we had. When we were kids we would daydream as a habit. Some of us spent more time daydreaming than actually being where we were. Teachers at times had to work to keep our attention, and we may have even been taught that daydreaming was bad. While it has its time and place, it remains one of the most important practices we need to maintain in the construction of the lives we want.

I had no idea what I wanted to do with my life. Perhaps I'm wrong but I do not think that most people at the age of 19 know what they want to do with their lives either. We go through this ticking time bomb of choices beginning in high school where the threat of "you will mess up your life" starts at such a young age ... as a result we either pick something to chase or we don't. Both are equally risky.

For me, "don't" was not an option ...What I knew was that I wanted to be happy. I wanted to have freedom and adventure and I wanted to feel good about myself. I aggressively pursued independence any way I could.

I grew up in a typical family, the middle daughter of three daughters with a father who was and still is the best definition of a hero that I've ever known. He was always working on something—my entire life. With a household of four ladies to keep happy, it's no wonder he was always busy with something.

I had weekly chores like any average kid and learned really young that if I wanted something I would have to work for it. I didn't resent this fact; I was empowered by it. Work was a normal part of our lives. We cut the lawn and trimmed the hedges, raked the leaves and shoveled snow, did the dishes, cleaned the bathrooms, learned to vacuum, dust and fold laundry. I helped my neighbor with her paper route when I was seven to earn extra money, and assisted my older sister in selling homemade, hand-painted clay necklaces at craft shows for a cut of the profits.

I started babysitting as soon as I was allowed, (after taking the proper courses in first aid, etc.), and gladly gave up any night that I could to earn the money that was available.

I applied for part-time jobs at the age of 14—jobs were almost impossible to find—but I lucked out with a kitchen job at a hospital when I was 15.

The Service Industry: My First "Profession"

I learned the service industry provided a great opportunity, so I worked my way up there. I started as a hostess in a family restaurant, while in high school, and quickly became envious of the tips I saw being left on the tables for the waiters and waitresses. I decided I needed to gain the chance and the confidence to become a waitress in order to get that opportunity for myself.

I still remember studying the menu and memorizing all of the side options and being scared during my first few shifts. As a server you either learn to get good and succeed or you don't get tips. The bigger the section you can handle, the more tips you make. The faster you can turn over tables, the more tips you make.

After some time I applied at a bar because of the exciting environment and big earning potential. I remember celebrating when I got hired at my first bar and the silly joke I had to tell to get the job!

Getting dressed up for work and hustling to keep customers' drinks full and my tips high! Then I dreamed of becoming a bartender, the Mecca in that industry. We were in awe of the bartenders … they were somehow higher than us … and they knew it too. Making drinks, managing the bar and tables and looking fancy—you had to be good.

At this time in my life I was going through a tough time. I was full of angst and anger as I felt misunderstood at home. I had moved out young in an effort to prove I could make it on my own and have no rules. As a result, my living situation was not a nice one. I lived in awful places because I could not afford anything nicer; I had a limited amount of choices to earn money as a teenager and admitting I needed help was not an option for me.

I was fiercely determined that I was going to somehow change my life and accomplish what the "lucky" people had. This fueled me, but I was a little bit like a heat-seeking missile.

Daring to find something to channel my energy into, I am so thankful today for the ethics and morals my parents instilled in me to clearly allow me the sense to choose which options were good ones, and which ones were not. Things could have turned out terribly had I made different choices.

I spent so much time imagining because my reality really "sucked." One of the biggest keys I learned when imagining the future was to picture myself winning, not losing, not doing so-so winning. I had to learn to see myself winning, guilt free, before it would ever happen anywhere else. This took time … It was as though there was an overwhelming exhaustion whenever I attempted to picture a successful future. Retraining my reactions, my imaginings, took time too. I had to learn to be positive and hopeful.

When I first began this exercise I struggled with seeing a perfect future. It was too egotistical to picture such success, so I pictured "survival"-oriented futures. I needed to give myself permission to succeed.

Somewhere in my early programming I attached the wrong things to my understanding of success. I needed to redefine this idea in order to have any hope at all of attaining it. In some cases I attached a certain amount of dishonesty to very successful people. I believed that in order for one person to succeed, someone else must fail; it was as though the success was directly responsible for the other person's failure like some warped version of yin and yang. I also think in my early programming I had attached the desire for material things to be the sign of a materialistic person. I had to recognize the polar differences in these characteristics and permit myself to honorably chase material success as well—and without apology.

I do not know where this programming came from, and it doesn't matter. What does matter is that I deleted it and wrote a new program to give myself permission to chase my dreams.

Playing "make believe" became a daily exercise for me. I was not where I wanted to be in my life, and the only way I got to spend time there was in my imagination. My challenge was figuring out how to translate my dreams into my reality. I was always in a rush to figure it out. I remember feeling "antsy" near the end of high school, desperate to start living large.

I dropped out of high school for a year to work two jobs because I needed the money and couldn't keep up my grades and earn enough at the same time. I saved enough to be able to stay on my own, and focus on school again, so I went back and studied hard enough to get accepted to a great university.

University

I applied at a nightclub near my university and got the job because of how I looked in hot pants, which at the time was fine with me. It was an amazing job to have at 19. The tips were unbelievable if you were good, and the nightlife was exactly what I wanted at that age. I bartended for a year, made killer money and got little sleep. However, I decided that it was a dangerous trap of a profession for me, so alluring, such an enchanting nightlife, such an intoxicating amount of money to be earned by committing to it, and days spent in recovery—I needed another plan.

When I was in university I wanted to win friends. I lived in the fine arts residence and was surrounded by amazingly talented people. When people asked me what I was talented at—I lied. Looking back on it now I realize it's because I was still insecure and counted on approval from others to build my self-esteem.

In an effort to win this approval while thinking there wasn't anything special about me, I made something up instead. The lie wasn't a big deal, I told people I had studied ballet at the National Ballet School, (my cousin dated someone who actually did; I guess this is where the story came from), and that got me some acceptance. I figured it was harmless.

Fast forward a month or so, and a girl from my high school had a class with a girl from my residence. They figured out I had lied and I will never forget the pleasure they took in outing me to anyone who would listen.

They loved catching me in this lie and really enjoyed the embarrassment it caused me. It passed quickly—no one really cared, but I have never forgotten those girls and how much they loved seeing someone "fail." I am truly thankful knowing that I have nothing in common with them in that department. I am also thankful for learning that who I am is only for me to judge; that my own approval is all I need.

At that stage in my life I was lost and looking for direction. Terrified of wasting more time and money only to end up graduating with a degree in "not what I want to do anymore," I flirted with the idea of taking another year off to work. I spent time in my playground and dreamed of a future that I loved.

I started to apply for office jobs in order to get some professional experience for my resume and also in an attempt to see if I was inspired by any career choice. I desperately couldn't wait to start to live a life of successful means.

I was totally insecure with who I was, and just beginning to navigate the definition of myself on my own without the influences of all of the people I grew up around. Learning who I was on my own was a daunting process.

I would spend time imagining myself in the future as a success. One of the best practices that I learned to do was to close my eyes and hit the fast-forward button in my mind. I'd ask myself, if I could picture my life in a perfect state five years from now, exactly what would that look like?

Then I would spend time imagining, creating, seeing the detail … allowing myself to win in my mind—win in all ways.

I would picture an incredibly happy future. One filled with security and adventure and love. Nice things adorned this future and the feeling of abundance always accompanied the trip into my imagination playground.

I was completely unmotivated at the concept of working for a big company and slowly trading my life for promotions. This is a great fit for many people. I am not judging the choice; however, it completely felt like prison to me. I was eager to throw myself into anything that would offer me what I was looking for. The problem I faced was that I had no idea what that was; I only knew what that wasn't.

Interviews: Failures and then Success

I went on interviews in the banking industry and with medical offices for administrative support and was shocked at how many of the male interviewers I sat before had inside them some kind of sexually suggestive comment. I could not picture myself being a "good girl" and fetching coffee for my bosses while they leered at me. Again, I am not suggesting that this is all companies—far from it—and I am not suggesting that this is the behavior of all men, again—far from it. It is simply the truth of what I experienced as a young university student who was aggressively job-seeking.

None of the options I found could compare in my mind to the service industry I was working in. I worked with amazing people, smart people, fun people and hard-working people. I just wanted something different. I wanted to learn more. I wanted to get better with people, lose my fear and get over my insecurities … where could I learn that? My search continued.

One day I went on a very different interview. The receptionist I spoke with was one of the most engaging people I had ever met in my life. She was bubbly and smart and really happy. The man that I interviewed with really talked with me and he too was also very happy. He was enthused about my experience and it was genuine. He asked if I was looking for something like office work, filing, phones, etc., or if I was looking for something more creative. I said something more creative, and he excitedly invited me to come back the next day for another interview … to see what the "creative" job was all about. I left that interview feeling more hopeful than I had felt in months.

The next day I returned and went on an interview by shadowing a sales rep. I was a little shocked at the idea that people actually still did door-to-door sales. I thought this concept died with my grandfather's generation. The sales rep talked to me about how people negotiate and how to read body language - things I had never even considered before, and I learned more in that one day than I had learned in years. To try it myself, however, was intimidating. The idea of being rejected sometimes so openly and so often, seriously scared me, but he told me he could teach me how to handle it.

I had so many questions it was the biggest clash of "airtime" I'd ever experienced. All of my fearful voices were chiming in with how crazy I would be to do this, but still, there was one really excited voice shouting at me to learn to be brave. The deciding factor for me was the money. We were to work completely on commission. To me this meant that I could get paid for how hard I worked—I wanted to learn how to do it.

I had to face one last interview before I got accepted and I was brought back to the office to sit before one of the most confident guys my own age I had ever met in my life. He was a manager at the age of 20—this blew my mind. He talked to me about expansion of their company and that they were not just looking for sales reps; that they were also looking for people to train to one day become managers and that I may eventually, if I was selected, have a chance to get some of this training—after I proved myself.

I wanted in. I wanted more than anything the chance to learn how to advance my life. I was prepared to do anything, (legal and moral, of course), to do this. The people in this place no longer spent time in their imagination playgrounds because they did not have to. They had learned a way to translate their dreams into a tangible plan to accomplish their goals. They had a vision.

I am so thankful for my years that I spent in my playground. My playground saved my life. My playground kept my hope alive.

Now I wanted to have and live my own vision.

Chapter 24

The Daredevil Inside

Julie

The only way through it is through it ~Julie

I knew I had a daredevil inside of me, I just knew it. We met face-to-face many times growing up. I was a fearless child, willing to jump off of anything no matter how high the stairs. I would climb the highest trees with the smallest branches just to get to the top. I would shimmy up the pole on the side of our two-story house to get on top of the roof when my parents weren't looking, just to slide back down the pole again. I would run through any dark scary woods on a dare, and we had 200 acres of dark scary woods. I would sneak past the security at any concert to get to the front row, and making my friends come with me. I was always the dare-devil, risk-taker amongst my friends and they reluctantly came with me most of the time. And that "most of the time," they always had fun.

I sneaked into, got into, and climbed up anything that seemed like there might be an adventure behind it. What's wrong with pushing the limit? Why waste a minute? And why waste time on what could have been or should have been because it might be too scary to try?

Ironically though, I never got into much trouble. Either I never got caught, I figured out a

way real fast to talk my way out of it, or maybe I just had a lot of divine intervention. Whatever the case, my plans were always for everyone to just have a fun, exciting time, no harm done. I detested boredom. I even detested a borderline-average, okay time. Life's too short. My mind was an adventure-seeking machine and I was determined to always figure out a way to do more.

Then one day in my early twenties, somehow, somewhere along the way, that daredevil became frightened. I'm not sure when or why or even how, but I do know that it was not during my normal routine. The physiological responses were undeniable and inescapable. I would experience the heart palpitations, the fatigue, the nausea, the chest pain, the shortness of breath and any other physiological response that can accompany anxiety. I started having panic attacks. And then I got mad.

"Why?" I wanted to know why! How could I suddenly be frightened in just a normal environment? Was it maybe the voice of reason speaking loudly to stop me from doing something dangerous? Had I finally entered a phase in my life that seemed scarier than anything else I ever experienced? I didn't know. I thought I was just living a normal college life. My mind would race almost uncontrollably to the point where I thought I was losing control.

And that was it … loss of control.

I was forced to come to grips with that idea years later when I realized it was control issues. The dissonance I felt between my brain and body taught me invaluable lessons that I will carry for the rest of my life. Because of the anxiety, it forced me to step up and face it, inevitably catapulting me to higher levels in my career and higher levels of understanding the world around me and really understanding myself. The alternative to stepping up was not an option.

In my early twenties I was about to graduate from college. It was my last semester and I was under quite a bit of stress. I broke up with my boyfriend, two of my grandparents had passed away within one month's time and I was working every night waiting tables. And I was taking a lot of hours to try and graduate, all the while pursuing my black belt in Tae Kwon Do.

Becoming an Adult

Why was I always in such a hurry? I didn't know. The anxiety would creep in and slowly form inside me. The harder I worked, the faster, I went. I was able to not focus on the inevitable, anxious feeling in my chest for brief moments in time. But the moment always arrived where I would remember again. That anxiety; those slow panic attacks were almost unbearable.

I was on my own for the first time, living a life in the jungle where all the normal, wild college animals roamed. I went to late night drive-thrus. I slept in with hangovers. I would rush to a final exam and then go out at night again.

I tried to wonder always what my life would be like and why did we have to make such a heavy decision at such a young age on what major or focus to choose in college. Who said that you are supposed to have your whole life planned out after high school?

I remembered growing up and how that may have shaped my existence. Someone told me once, "Think about what you wanted to be growing up. That gives you a clear indication of what your path should be in life." I thought back and remembered watching the Olympics when Nadia Comaneci won the gold medal representing Romania in the gymnastics tournament, scoring seven perfect tens. I was six.

I remember watching her fly through the air on the parallel bars. She was so majestic, so magical. She was what I wanted to be. I would race to watch her on TV as the network would play her performance in slow motion again and again over the next months and years with the tune from the popular soap opera, *The Young and The Restless*, a tune I later learned to play at my piano recital, a tune that was later titled "Nadia's theme." I played that image in my head over and over again.

That was me. I was going to win the gold medal for the USA one day in gymnastics. I wanted to look like, dress like, and walk like Nadia. So much so, I convinced my mom to buy me a leotard that was the same color as hers and I would wear it every day in the summer with my hair pulled back. When no one was looking, I would stand like her in the way she did when she would pounce in her landing, with the lower back exaggeratedly arched and shoulders pulled back and stomach protruding.

"Stand up straight Julie! Why are you standing that way?" My mother would say to me and make me stand against the wall until I straightened.

I could not tell her my secret. She didn't know that she was talking to the future USA gold medal gymnast, the best one that ever existed in the history of the world. I was practicing my stance.

I would go out on the front lawn and do cartwheels all day long until my hands grew blisters. The closest thing we had to parallel bars at my house were the pecan trees out in our back yard. So, of course, I climbed them all and tried to jump from limb to limb, which I did everyday and all the time until I fell out and broke my left arm. It happened on Mother's Day. And for that, "Mom, I'm sorry."

I was rushed to the hospital and the doctor cut my leotard off my arm with a pair of giant black scissors. I didn't even care that my arm was broken. I was just devastated about my leotard. I never told my mom why that leotard was so special to me, but I guess I threw that dream away in the garbage can along with the leotards. I clearly needed gymnastic lessons.

Once the cast was removed, my mom decided that I should take piano instead. Because my uncle was a concert pianist and brilliant musician, I sat down next to him every Tuesday afternoon at four o'clock at his baby grand and proceed to take lessons for the next six years.

We had a very old, very used, and very out-of-tune piano where the keys would stick together, and this is what I had to practice on at home. I tried, I practiced, I learned how to play the chords and read the music. I got by but I wasn't great. There was no magical talented musical gift in my tiny little third-grade fingers.

Nadia's Theme

But then, one day, I did find in one of my uncle's dusty piano books, "Nadia's Theme," and I begged him to teach me. I played it for hours and hours and I would play it in slow motion, visualizing my face on Nadia's body as she was on those balance beams. I would close my eyes and play. That was me, I was her. I could fly. That was about the height of my musical career. After many rotations around the sun and many recitals later, my mom finally realized that I wasn't Liberace and released me from the chambers.

She taught me to cook and sew instead.

I grew up in an interesting house. It was antique and was occupied by Yankee troops during the Civil War. It was used as a hospital for their dying and wounded soldiers. Two hundred years later, it was occupied by my family and me. It was known to be haunted and I, along with my three brothers, have our long list of midnight stories. Intriguing as it was, I didn't feel like I had a normal childhood living in that house. Although, what is normal? Growing up in a household with only brothers and only male cousins, I tried to learn how to be tough and stand out.

My father was in the Peace Corps and he had tons of relics hanging in his study. He had machetes and bow and arrows hanging on the wall from some of the tribes he lived with. He had tons of pottery and statues and even had what he claimed was a real shrunken head. My friends came over just to touch it.

Although he never hunted, my father taught me to shoot a rifle by the time I was eight. I was good. I learned how to hit the target every time.

We had a farm with chickens, goats, cattle, and geese. We also had a pond in our back yard, and often fished for catfish with bamboo poles and crickets for bait. I learned to have a deep affinity for animals and for all living creatures, even the bugs, spiders, lizards, and snakes that shared our yard. Maybe that's why today, I don't eat meat. I just don't like it.

My parents had books shelves of eclectic books ranging from the US presidents, to Machu Picchu Indians, to understanding the Dow Jones report, to vampire fairy tales, to caring for your green house, and of course, the Holy Bible. I remember reading them all.

One day, in my late teens, a friend of my parents drove a red convertible Porsche to our house and I found out that she was a stockbroker. I looked at her car and said to myself, "I want that life; I want that car."

As so it began. In my right hand I held the book of transcendental meditation and in my left, the Wall Street Journal. I was going to pursue a career in Finance and Business, run a business, be the greatest stock broker that ever existed and save the world and lead them to peace all at the same time while playing "Nadia's Theme" in my head.

A little over-indulgent, I realize now. I lost interest in the stock broking career somewhere along the way. But looking back, I realized that even then, at such a tender age, that something inside was pointing me to the great balance in life. You can have an abundant career, a great family and listen to your soul all at once and don't need to sacrifice one to have the other.

After graduating college, the panic attacks persisted. I started having dreams that I was floating out in space all alone with nothing to hold on to and nothing but infinity in all directions. I guess I felt lost, with no control. The best thing I could think of besides going a million miles an hour to escape was to start meditating and praying. It helped me to control my breathing and concentrate from the inside out. I started gaining the support of my thoughts and really tried to align them with my heart. It helped a great deal and really drove me to start concentrating on myself.

A Career: How, When and Where?

I started reading books on health and wellness, on how the mind and brain work, and on self- therapy. These helped me find stillness within. It didn't always last and took a lot of practice, but I desperately needed some inner peace in my life.

Along the way, I answered an ad in the paper. I was looking to start a career, not sure where to go. I had just spent the last four and a half years of my life studying Finance and Math while waiting tables to survive, taking Tae Kwon Do, and doing some modeling on the side. I felt like I really had no direction. I liked business; I always felt in my heart that I wanted to run my own business, but no idea or concept on how to even start something like that.

I found an ad in the paper, called and went in for an interview.

Although I was still battling with panic attacks, there was no way I was going to allow that to stop me.

I had to find my daredevil …

THE FIELD

Julie and Michell

Boot Camp

Formal education will make you a living;
self education will make you a fortune. —**Jim Rohn**

Opportunity does not knock, it presents itself
when you beat down the door. —**Kyle Chandler**

Michell

Both of us started a door-to-door, commission-only position. We quickly learned about self- motivation and confidence … or our lack of it.

The field was the best professor I've ever met.

I was anxious whenever I had to talk to people that I didn't already know, like the receptionist at the doctor's office or friends of friends that I just met. Learning to overcome this fear was the biggest challenge I had faced yet in my young life.

My first day in the field, I was too afraid to speak to anyone. Finally my trainer literally left me on someone's doorstep by physically running away so that I would have no choice but to speak. I stumbled my way through my sales presentation and survived the terror of that first sales call. I am eternally grateful to the man whom I was speaking to. He could see how afraid I was and honestly did most of the talking himself. He signed himself up for our service in an effort, I am sure, to boost the confidence of this terrified little girl he saw before him … I will never forget his kindness.

At every door after him I learned something. I learned what made people laugh and what did not. I learned to read facial expressions and body language and tone and eye movements and a thousand tiny little things that we do as people when we are communicating. I was fascinated by what I was learning.

Door to Door

I quickly learned that I was not great at negotiating or handling rejection or even really listening, for that matter. I learned that I got discouraged more easily than I expected and that I would lose my attitude quickly, but I wanted to get better. Overcoming these challenges would lead me to a different level of life, and I was not going to back down until I learned to get better.

In the office, the managers talked about being positive by choice, and learning to be confident because you believe in yourself and all kinds of crazy things, things that I had never really heard people talk about that much. My reaction was a little bit "they must be on Prozac" as I'd never been surrounded by such positivity on purpose before. Some other reps quit because they thought it was wrong for the managers to tell people they could learn to succeed at something like this, that it was wrong to get people's hopes up … I *wanted* to get my hopes up.

The months that followed truly changed my life. I learned about setting goals—picking a direction on purpose and then committing to the pursuit of these things—and how much of an impact it made on my daily performance.

I learned about negotiating by doing something daily that we called practice pitching. The intent was not to learn how to "mess" with the customer; it was to learn how to talk with them … To honestly talk without nervousness, insecurity, feeling inferior—just talk. To be able to look people in the eye and not be afraid of what they will say. Going through this process was a challenge for me because of all of the insecurities I had inside of myself. Along with the daily practice and coaching sessions in the morning, we then went out into the field to sell. Every day was different. Some days were good days and some days were bad days. I was determined to learn how to stay consistent. I realized that the work required was to be done inside of me, not out in the field. When I lost my confidence or forgot my reason for working so hard, my results went away too.

I started to read every self-help book I could get my hands on. I devoured stories on attitude and success and perspective and truly felt infected with the changes that were occurring within me. I came back to the office and was greeted by others who wanted to encourage and support me. I had found a place where people actually took the time to teach me and support me like nowhere else I'd ever gone.

I was fortunate to find some incredible mentors during this time, mentors that changed my life. The biggest one for me was a beautiful and tough-as-nails girl from Seattle; she was absolutely fearless. She spoke her mind, could public speak in front of a room and captivate them and honestly understood how to teach. I was in awe of her from the beginning.

She taught me how to be confident as a woman in business, and the spirit inside of her was the brightest I had ever met. The six months that I spent working with her is what equipped me for the next six years of my career. We worked door-to-door together. She taught me about people. She humbled me about my attitude. She made me realize that I had a lot of work to do to *become* self-confident instead of *acting* confident. And then she helped me begin that process. I do not know what my life would have looked like if I had not been so fortunate as to find this amazing teacher so early in my professional life.

To me the time I spent in the field was such a time of discovery. I respected all of us who had the courage to even try to succeed at it. It was fierce at times. Different cities have different personalities, and different products get received differently. We worked with some crazy teams of people. The common characteristic was the amazing energy. We were ambitious. We were excited and yes, we worked on commission and were a little crazy.

Understanding that the opportunity in front of us was, simply put, a chance. We had three choices: decide if it wouldn't be possible; wait for a prettier opportunity to show up; or, get busy and give everything we had to make this one work.

Today I still believe that the field is the most valuable experience anyone can give themselves. Not online connecting, not text conversations … real people. Face to face negotiation—there is only one way to learn this … and it is to do it.

When you're in the field you learn the truth, the truth about you and people. I call it "the amazing truth."

People generally will act and react towards you the way you act and react towards them first.

Learning to connect with people and become a great communicator will change your life.

Realizing how strong you are enables you to dream bigger.

Developing a work ethic that is unbreakable will serve all future endeavors, and learning to take the word "no" with grace and still stay focused, gives you the ability to play at your best under pressure.

Julie

You'll never become a millionaire in the field. But what the field teaches you is a millionaire's secrets.

My first few weeks in the field were exhausting. I was mentally, physically and emotionally tired. My feet hurt, my brain hurt, my throat hurt. Do I have to say this pitch one more time? My dreams at night were exhausting. I was still in the field in my dream, pitching the same customer over and over and over again. He didn't know what I was talking about or what I was trying to sell. Then I would wake up and start pitching again. Then I would wake up again. Was that a dream within a dream?

I never heard so many no's in my life. Lots and lots of no's were surrounding me. Rejection was everywhere. I realized that I was terrified to talk to some people. In fact, the first business I walked into, I heard the record scratch - in my head that is. Everyone looked up at me in what I thought was slow motion and the room went silent. I just stared.

I felt the blood rising in my face—so fast and hot. I could suddenly hear the intense rhythm of my heart beat. "Oops, wrong business," I said, in a very high pitched voice and jumped out and back onto the sidewalk as fast as possible … Deep breaths.

"Oh God, I will never get through this!" "Yes I will." "No you can't."

I battled. I told everyone that morning that I was going to have the best day ever! I committed out loud to all my peers that I was going to beat everyone today. Oh, how I felt like a loser. I knew that the only way through it was to keep going. So I forced myself to continue. Do I really have to go back to the office and tell everyone how horrible I was in the field?

Then suddenly, something happened. Someone bought … What?? Yes, that happened, and the sun was shining again. My confidence reappeared and was high.

In the beginning, when someone just looked at me, I expected them to say no. My approach was to get as many no's as possible so that I can prove that this doesn't work. I would almost say to them, "You don't want this, right?" so that I didn't have to hear another no. Was I invading their privacy?

Once I got over the fear, frustration entered. I saw others doing it and being successful. Why can't I? If I didn't learn how to take the rejection, I would crumple up and die. I made myself have no choice. I would put one step in front of the other and just open my mouth to talk to complete strangers. I can depend on me, right? Again, I made myself have no choice. If I didn't figure it out, no one was going to do it for me.

I learned a lot about myself those first few weeks, a lot that I never really realized or was in denial about. I was terrified of being judged.

I was terrified to hear the word "no." I was terrified that I wouldn't perform. I was terrified that I wouldn't match up to my peers. It was hot outside, and I was knocking on doors. Did I really reach a low?

I saw a lot of people come in and then quit.

None of this sounds glamorous, I know. That's not my intention. But what I quickly realized was that none of this had anything to do with sales. It had everything to do with me learning to be focused and goal-driven. I had to learn to communicate and ask for things that I wanted, and not let obstacles stop me. I had to learn that rejection just meant "next"—that something better was waiting in the future for me to show up.

I found what my potential was in the field. I found out about me. It was scary and great all at once. Through great challenge, I stood up. I was put to the test and I followed through.

I know now that if I had backed down from such a great challenge, I would have regretted it. I also know that those fears in the field were all inside of me and all created and designed by me. I also know that all those people I thought were judging me were a reflection of my own self-image. And it was about me learning how to fail, to succeed, and to push myself.

I didn't realize any of this until much later. It was never about the sales. I realized that this whole position was disguised, for me. It was a boot camp for my soul. If I couldn't break my comfort zone and figure this out, I would continually be challenged throughout my life.

My thinking in the beginning was amateur and immature. I was money-hungry, results driven, hyper-focused and expected excellence from everyone around me. I forced myself to be bold, and with the highest integrity I practiced to be the best. I worked with an extreme sense of urgency and intensity and needed to be number one. I was frustrated when those around me didn't live up to my standard of work ethic. I felt I wanted it more for those around me than they wanted it for themselves.

On paper and in business, I did extraordinarily well. I was promoted in record time, with a large team of people that I had personally trained.

On the inside, I was terrified. I was terrified to succeed. I was terrified to speak in public. I was terrified to recite my personal goals in front of a room. I was unsure of almost everything I was doing. I was just closing my eyes and running, which was the same advice I gave to others when I didn't know the answer. I felt as though I was moving so quickly, that I couldn't keep up.

But I did it anyway.

Looking back on my first six months in the field, and all the things I had to personally learn about myself, I realized a lot about myself. I realized I learned more in those six months than I had in the previous ten years.

I am completely convinced, now, sixteen years later, after working with thousands of people who I've seen go through the field, that everyone, everywhere, should experience this. It is not easy and it is not glamorous. But, you'd be quite surprised at what you may find out about yourself. For most, it is a tough realization of what our true character needs.

For me, I was quite humbled …

Chapter 26

FOOTPRINTS IN THE SNOW

Michell

When I got promoted to be the Assistant Manager of the sales office I was working in, my manager took me on a $500 shopping spree for "interviewing" clothes. I had never experienced such generosity outside of my family before in my life. When I was going through the field I bought most of my business clothes from Goodwill as that was what my budget could afford. After all, business clothes were expensive, and my "I won't conform" attitude argued against dressing like a corporate girl. Now that I was expected to learn to conduct interviews for job seekers, and that I was only 20 years old and looked about 14, my manager didn't really give me a choice.

We went to a few outlet stores that I liked and loaded up a change room full of skirts and blouses, jackets and pants; everything you could imagine I needed—I needed. I literally was wearing a pair of men's dress pants secured with a safety pin in the back because I liked the style of the cut way better than the women's high-wasted, tapered options of the early '90s.

We left that store with four bags of clothes. He then took me to get a couple pairs of shoes and a briefcase of my own. I didn't recognize myself—in a good way. I am still overwhelmingly thankful for his generosity in investing in me. He saw potential in me to succeed in business that I had not comprehended yet. I figured that I would simply dress up and play business girl every day, and the game of "make believe" would continue.

Conducting interviews literally kicked me in the stomach. I was so intimidated to walk out into that lobby and pick up the resume of the next candidate that I honestly got physically sick because of my fear. There were hundreds of interviews to be conducted every week; we were in the middle of a recession and job seekers were plentiful. It was a different time then too; no one had a cell phone, the internet did not exist, and the only business directory was the yellow pages. Interviewing was a whole different ballgame.

As a young girl who had not yet gained her confidence in this environment, every interview was a more horrifying experience than the last. People took control of me in the interview, over and over again. My voice was shaky and I couldn't focus on the questions I meant to ask because I was so afraid of what they all thought. I felt terrible as it became obvious to me that many of the people coming in for interviews would never get offers from us due to their lack of skills, and I knew they needed to work. Whatever confidence I had built through my conquering of the field, I quickly lost. This next level of performance seemed too daunting for me to tackle.

Our office administrators were like superwomen. They organized everybody's schedules, answered a six-line phone system like champs and were the most cheerful people I had ever experienced—amidst all of the chaos. They would see the tears getting ready to spill from my eyes and pull me into the kitchen to give me encouragement. They'd constantly reiterate to me that I deserved the position I had earned. I had the right to be interviewing all of these people. But I was so far out of my comfort zone I couldn't even find a shadow of myself.

Every day was like a giant beating, but my manager would not let me quit. He told me that the only way that I was going to learn to stop letting people intimidate me was to stop letting people intimidate me. That when I got tired of losing control, I would start to stay in control, and that it was my decision to stay uncomfortable or to learn to get comfortable in this new role. I resented him at the time.

I finally started to gain control when I got mad. I was mad at the number of times an interview looked me up and down in an unprofessional way when I called out his name from the resume. I was mad that some of the women I interviewed challenged my title with the company with a knowing look on their faces. I was mad at the other male manager in the office and how he compared his successful results at interviewing with all of my failures. I was mad that he suggested that women shouldn't interview. I was mad at myself for feeling scared, and I was mostly mad at myself for thinking that maybe they were all right … that I was crazy to think that a young lady could and would succeed at building a company based on her own work ethic, commitment and results. Apparently "mad" was what I needed.

I made a decision. I wasn't asking permission for approval anymore, and I wasn't going to let anyone make me doubt myself again. If I had to roll the dice on one person in my life, it was going to be me. I was finished with the unsure little girl show and was ready for the "get out of my way" show to start. I think I was a little sharp around the edges for a while, and I spoke with a bit of an "I dare you" in my voice, but I needed to manifest my confidence somehow, and this is how it showed up for me.

Interviews stopped looking at me like a kid because I stopped thinking they would see me that way. What a major feat it was for me to conquer that insecurity. I had been the punching bag for a world of unemployed, upset people for months … No more.

Overcoming this challenge was one of the biggest tests I'd ever faced at this point in my life. It took me a year to go through this process, interviewing close to 50 candidates a day, five days a week for almost a year, before I beat it. That's a lot of hits to take along the way. It made me strong though, and that strong girl needed that strength for what came next.

Finally My Own Business

Every step forward was equally exciting and scary. After learning to run the office as a manager, I opened my company in September of 1996, three days before my 23rd birthday.

My sales reps and I were a group of motivated, hardworking people who were in it to win. Our entire focus was building our sales force and expanding by opening more businesses.

The next year was a blur of interviews, motivational meetings, strategy sessions, paperwork, challenges and victories. I was a rookie and I made a ton of mistakes. Some of those mistakes cost us dearly,

I lost my sales force as a result of some of those mistakes, and the day came when things weren't going well at all—again.

I'm not sure I ever remember becoming instantly more afraid in my life with the realization. All of what we had spent years building was falling apart.

I packed up my rental house and moved into my office to save money. No one knew that I was living there in the industrial park with my cat and I didn't plan for anyone to find out either. It was scary. I slept on the floor behind my desk with a crowbar beside me, just in case. I had a shower in the office and an old television set that I had traded for an *Ani DiFranco* CD in university. There was a blockbuster video within walking distance that had a cheap, used movies bin and I spent the rest of my time alone with all of my books learning how to get better, encouraging myself to keep fighting.

Struggling to rebuild my business was tougher than building it the first time. I had to get people excited about something that I was struggling to be excited about myself; I had lost sight of my goals. I felt like I was depleting every last ounce of energy inside myself to attempt to do this. It was exhausting beyond belief. Maintaining your faith in something when it's wavering is the most draining of endeavors to take on. Holidays were tough. Spending the long Thanksgiving Weekend in an abandoned industrial park alone is an experience I would never wish on anyone … Or Christmas … Or New Year's Eve.

In the winter it was a little trickier to keep my secret safe. When it snowed overnight and my reps arrived in the morning, they would know I hadn't left the night before as the snow had not been cleared. I remember the first snowfall and the immediate panic I felt to make sure it looked like I arrived early that morning. I put on my parka and winter boots and trudged all the way down to the corner of the street and back again to ensure it looked like people had been busy at my office, and no one would see the solitude that I was experiencing.

After I had been living there for a year, Alison, a dear friend of mine wanted to move back to Toronto and work with me, so she moved into the office too. We slept on a leather sectional couch with our feet meeting in the middle and lived on the snack machines in our lobby. We were both a little lost but unwilling to give up, and so we fought through the storm together. That industrial park became a whole lot more like an adventure, once I wasn't there alone anymore. It's amazing what you can get through when you have someone there who stands together with you. It's amazing too, the things we saw, peeking out the windows in the middle of the night …

Months continued to pass, and we kept barely surviving—but we laughed, and we planned and we dreamed, believing we would one day actually win. With an absence of money, our dreams are what fed us, so we were full to the brim and almost exploding with excitement for that "one day" to come … We had a freezer full of frozen pizza that we were trying to sell and a microwave (yuck) to cook them in … we would be fine.

There were a lot of "uncontrollables" that I was terrible at handling, and while I learned, we struggled.

But I eventually did learn, and the ocean liner started to turn around again …

Months later I was able to finally move out of the office, but the lessons I learned through this time of struggle I owe the rest of my success to. What I learned then is still what fuels me now.

I never would have had this strength if the footprints hadn't been required.

I learned that I won't cheat and I don't quit. There's a ton of self-respect in that.

Chapter 27

Freedom Drive

Julie

I moved to Charlotte, North Carolina, to open my sales and marketing business. I was only 24. My goal was to grow the biggest sales force in North Carolina and expand all throughout the United States. I had huge goals.

I found an office space, which happened to be on Freedom Drive. It was definitely not the most elegant part of town, but it was cheap. It was a stand-alone brick building with a giant dumpster by the front door; there were two offices, a lobby, a meeting room and a warehouse. The carpet had eternal runs and coffee stains. The walls were paper-thin, there was one tiny bathroom, and I was sharing space with another business owner that brought his slobbering, 250 pound Mastiff to work every day. I did love that dog.

I shared the administration. My administrator, whom I adored, had a brand new baby and no babysitter, so she brought her beautiful little girl to work every day and had her up at the front desk with her.

I was ready for business!

My first step was to recruit. I needed to fill my office with tons of sales reps to work the city and satisfy my clients. I had what we called a "lister." The lister actually signed the clients for my business. The lister would pitch several restaurants, golf courses, or auto shops in the area to allow us to sell discounted prices for their places and to drive traffic through their doors. When he signed the deal, we sold the services to consumers. The consumers would purchase the discounted rates and we hoped that they would become a patron to that business.

Every day I showed up at that location on Freedom Drive at 7:00 a.m. Every night I would leave that location on Freedom Drive at 10:00 p.m. In the morning I held sales trainings, my own version of inspirational meetings, goal setting circles and workshops. During the day, I interviewed at least 20 people a day and then would meet the reps in the field to help train them or make some extra cash before we went back to the office to settle up for the day.

I realized much later how important image was to the growth of my business. I'm not quite sure what potential candidates must have thought at the time, entering that building. I sometimes wore sunglasses on my head and chewed gum during the interviews. What did I know? I sometimes left my lunch on the desk, had overflowing garbage, and paperwork strewn throughout the office during my interviews. The dog roamed around a lot, the baby cried quite often, and my office was certainly never clutter-free. I didn't know that it mattered, as simple as that concept was.

I was just too busy trying to make my business grow to realize that it wasn't.

Losing My Grip

Besides the three main things I knew I had to do … which were showing up, interviewing for new sales reps every day, and going to the field to make extra money … there was nothing else! I didn't have any other plan.

I had no schedule, I kept really disorganized records, I was terrified everyday to stand up in front of my office and speak about goals and opportunity, I didn't know how to keep stats for my administration, my office was a dump, and I thought I had to be this gigantic, fearless leader for all of these people.

When my reps came back with excuses piled up, I implemented no standards and let them feel as though it was okay.

I had no money. My beat up Mercury Cougar had used tires that I got from the junkyard up the street for $20 each and they kept blowing out on me every couple of weeks. The heater and air conditioner were out of commission and only the driver's side window rolled down. Sometimes the window just fell down into the door and I had to bring it in to the mechanic to fish it out. It was really cold during the winter.

I was completely stressed out and made zero time for myself. I wore eye glasses at the time, and one of the screws on the left handle fell out, so I got the bright idea of taping it together until I got them fixed. One day as I was conducting an interview, I moved forward and my glasses fell off to the side and just hung on my right ear.

I don't really know what a nervous breakdown means, but in the middle of the winter that year, I broke down in tears, and I think I cried for one month straight.

I met my doomsday. Truly, it was more like I met my "doomsyear." With giant expectations for me and my team, we had moved to Charlotte with one goal in mind. We were going to be the best. I put everything I had learned into play. This was it; my time to shine. For those 12 months, I did nothing but struggle. I was losing money, I was losing faith in my abilities and who I was, and I was losing my confidence. Mostly, I felt like I let my team down.

I was lost again, floating in space, making things up to make some sense of the disoriented life I was leading. What do I say; where do I go? Is this a good goal to shoot for? Why am I here? Where is my family? I felt so alone—that creepy-crawly anxiety crept back in again. I resorted to tears and frustration. My giant expectations had been crushed by a Mac truck and I felt like that little six-year-old girl again back in the hospital facing those big, black, giant scissors.

I was just so far out of my comfort zone and with absolutely no plan or strategy to move forward. I was showing up everyday doing the same thing hoping that something would change.

That is Albert Einstein's definition of insanity.

I had to learn to understand my emotions and try to change, based on fact and experience, passion and desire, not anger and fear. Although fear is one of the strongest emotions, it is the one that offers the least results. Once the negative emotion is gone, so are the negative actions.

Exactly one year from the day I opened in Charlotte, I was offered an opportunity to work down in Miami. I'm thankful that I didn't quit before that. I am thankful that I was able to change my environment.

I am thankful because this is where my life changed once again.

Chapter 28

Space Mountain

Julie and Michell

Blast off on a journey into outer space on this classic attraction. Board a sleek, rocket-shaped vehicle in the glow-in-the-dark Space Port and begin a steady climb up the 180-foot high mountain, passing the Mission Control booth and myriad pulsating lights along the way.

Once at the top, feel the wind race across your face as you are propelled through the remote blackness of the dark universe—illuminated only by shooting stars, celestial satellites, spinning black holes and shimmering constellations—during a rip-roaring rocket ride through the farthest reaches of time and space. —**Space Mountain**

Michell

The first thing I did was buy a bed. We moved out of the office after a year and a half. I was so scared to spend any money that it was only after putting over $100,000 back in the bank that I felt comfortable to finally pay for a rental house again. The day we moved in, I went to the best mattress store around and asked for the best king size bed they had—I spent $4000 on the mattress alone.

For two nights we slept on the floor of our own bedrooms without any furniture, just happy to have a bedroom to be in again. We took Alison's car to Wal-Mart to pick up supplies for our new house and it died in the parking lot, once and for all. It was stuck in third gear and was super dangerous to operate; she bought it for only $400 after all—it was her pizza mobile and it was a gem. We bought a beautiful love seat from a fancy furniture shop and the biggest TV we could carry.

Our next destination was Ikea. We loaded up my brand new custom-ordered jeep until it was full, and piled so many boxes of bookcases and cabinets on top that we got terrified looks from all of the people walking by as they watched us "twine" it all up on the roof … seriously, almost three feet high—so dangerous. With four-way flashers on, I drove back to our new house at about 40 km per hour, with both of us holding onto the twine to keep it tight. That was one of the happiest car rides I've ever had.

Within the next two years those first four offices turned into 30 offices and we were 700 people strong in the field every day. Our supplier had signed contracts with several new clients who were well branded and had deep pockets for their marketing budgets. We were working on four projects at the same time with a huge opportunity for growth. We had one campaign where we staffed booths signing up customers for credit cards. We had a team selling telecom services residentially, another team selling membership cards for local restaurants, and a team selling home alarm systems. We were busy! There were managers earning insane incomes and people recruiting all of their friends.

There was a fever surrounding all of the success that was happening. We had certainly paid our dues but we were now riding the opposite tide—that of plenty and felt as though we had done it all on our own. My previous experience had taught me well to save my money, and save I did. When I took my weekly commission cheques in to the bank, the tellers almost always reacted in shock. The machine had been built and while it lasted it was almost like a money press with a license to run nonstop.

We attended conferences with other sales teams across North America and were part of something that was far bigger than even I had imagined. I remember taking two coach buses down to Madison Square Garden to attend an awards conference that blew my mind.

The next year we went to Philadelphia and attended another one with over 5,000 people doing the same thing we were doing. Michael Buffer, the famous voice of the boxing ring, started the conference off with his trademark call of "Let's get ready to rumble," and other celebrities sat on stage as special guest-speakers. I had wanted more than anything to accomplish that kind of success in my own life.

As business owners contracted by this supplier, we got to attend a special R and R weekend every year and these too blew my mind. The resorts we stayed at were luxurious beyond my imagination. My first one was in Palm Springs and there were mist jets at the outdoor bar which let off ice-mist blasts every so often to ensure we didn't get too hot while we drank.

Five diamond resorts, recognition for our accomplishments, so many successful people—we were in the greatest business in the world. I did not doubt this for a second. I had won the lottery the day I made the decision to work on commission, and I could not believe my luck in the great fortune of finding that kind of a job.

We attended seminars to help us be more successful business owners and learn how to improve our skills as managers, leaders, and coaches. The information was like a drug. The more we learned the better we did. These meetings were held all over North America in places like Los Angeles, Chicago and Miami—this was impressive enough to me! I stood in line at customs and giggled to myself that I had checked off the "business" box on my immigration card as the reason for travelling. After the first year of running my business, I was asked to be one of the speakers at these meetings—which terrified me as much as it excited me. Who would believe I was a real business woman? I still just dressed up and played "business girl" every day, and I was learning to get better.

Sales continued to grow and so did my sales force. I was on the fast track and was beginning to get more and more recognition amongst my peers. I thirsted for more direction so as to continue growing my business. One day a fancy invitation arrived for me at the office; my company's supplier was hosting a meeting in Las Vegas! It was for the "rising stars." I called my travel agent the second I received it. This is where I met Julie for the first time.

Julie

And because the majority of the attraction takes place in the dark, you just never know which way you are going to turn or drop!

—Space Mountain

Boy, does that say it all—a rip-roaring rocket ride through the dark and you just never know which way you are going to turn or drop!

When success hit, it came fast. It was like some unbelievable locomotive revving up its engine over and over, putt-putting to start, spitting and coughing out the pieces of coal that didn't burn to produce the steam needed to drive the engine. But once it finally kicked in, that self- propelled engine didn't stop.

I remember my trip to Las Vegas. It was called a Rising Star event. Our supplier sent out invitations to business owners that met their "Rising Star" criteria. I was a big shot! My business was at an all-time high, I was banking a ton of money, I had expanded my organization of sales offices to over five different states, and I was going to Las Vegas!

I remember meeting Michell there. She was considered a powerhouse in Canada and there was big talk about all the things she was doing and accomplishing. Every one of our mentors had been trying to arrange for the two of us to meet. I introduced myself first. I found out that she started her business in Canada at approximately the same time, three years earlier. We both had taken very similar paths.

What a weekend! We played blackjack for the first time, we took a helicopter ride over the strip, and we watched the latest version of O, spent half of our days in the spa and the other half buying Gucci bags. I think we slept about three hours that entire weekend at our six star resort. What else would two single, 20-something girls do in Las Vegas, with wads of money in our pockets?

I barely made it back to my Miami office Monday morning—but I made it, with a big smile on my face.

The years to follow were similar; limo rides in the cities of our events, speaking engagements where we stood up to speak at times in front of thousands. I remember running up to the stage at one of our supplier's most prestigious award ceremonies to my favorite song at the time, Christina Aguilara's *Fighter*.

I needed a new car, and I remember going to the dealership to buy a new one with cash.

At one of our supplier's events, Joe Theisman, the football legend, was speaking. I was taken from the crowd to go back stage and have a photo taken with him. I remember standing behind the curtain waiting, and there was Michell, waiting for the same thing. We looked at each other and giggled.

Yes, we were riding the rollercoaster. In recognition of each of our network's sales growth we were both appointed to consultant roles with our supplier within a month of each other. We were the first two women to ever accomplish this within their organization.

The Tsunami

Then the tsunami hit. The tsunami, in every sense of the word came crashing down on my world. With a changing economy and higher competition with cheaper vendors, our clients decided to cut commissions, tighten the reins on existing products, and pull away some of the products we were selling. In some parts of the country we decided to change clients all together and in other parts we decided to try to figure out a way to make it work.

The changes were drastic and I wasn't prepared to handle what was about to come. When things are great and life feels at an all time high, it's hard to ever think that something can come to a screeching halt. There were a lot of casualties from the change. And because I had been speeding in overdrive in one direction for so long, changing gears was a foreign language to me. I lost my attitude and my confidence, didn't know how to give the proper direction, and my ability to adapt to a new way of thinking was so amateur, that I suffered the consequences.

Luckily I had saved a lot of money.

Having, by then, seven straight years of upward success is a lot to brag about. And Michell had the same.

Of course we made a million mistakes, and a lot of that time we were just closing our eyes and running. We didn't have a lot of answers for a lot of the people on our teams. In fact, we grew so fast, in our separate countries, that we didn't know how to stop and we didn't have time for anything or anyone else, including ourselves. With client shifts and managers moving from one place to the next, I lost focus … and I lost confidence.

I kept doing everything I knew how to do, along with patchwork and Band Aids, but I had no answers. It was like taking a growing tree with tons of fruit and shaking it as hard as you possibly could. In fact, it was like a hurricane blowing through that tree, where most of the fruit falls off. I hung on with all my might and I didn't let go and neither did the "fighters."

The strongest people on my team survived our tsunami, and together, slowly, and over the years, we rebuilt Rome. I am so thankful and grateful for the strength and support of my team at that time, as we went blindly forward just like riding Space Mountain.

During a lot of that time, I didn't feel like much of a leader. My perspective was different, I was humbled and learning a ton of life lessons.

In Canada, Michell experienced her own tsunami, with incredibly similar events. Unexpected challenges were met by inexperienced young entrepreneurs who couldn't find a solution before we lost our sales force. When watching years of work being washed away in one crashing occurrence and putting the pieces back together again after the last of the waves died out, it's amazing how quiet it gets after the storm. It is even more amazing rebuilding with the people who survive it with you.

It was only after the crash that that we both began to realize what true leadership was all about. That in only suffering the complete comprehension of failure and losing people as a cost of that failure, we spoke from our hearts and admitted our mistakes. Having the courage to stand strong and do it again, but different and better the next time, required bravery. To lead when you know the damage of defeat is something respected and known only by the battle scarred.

Over the next few years, both of our organizations grew, bigger than they had ever been before, bigger than perhaps we'd even ever imagined.

Just like in any business, we expected there to be highs and lows but we just did not realize that we were in the extreme sports version of entrepreneurial business play, where the highs and lows were intergalactic ... and we were addicted to the game.

Chapter 29

INTO THE GREAT WIDE OPEN

Julie and Michell

For the past ten years we've been conspiring.

Dreaming, planning and plotting our next endeavors.

We started looking at our life experiences as the new beginning for the next adventure creating a hit list, answering that powerful first question, and endeavoring to acquire it together. We got really clear on what we both want. We won't quit until we get it.

Finding ways to serve others while honoring the industry that has given us so much has become our new commitment. We want to give back as we've received so much.

Surviving Space Mountain alone but together, bonded our friendship in a way that can only be described as soul sisters … We both feel proud, of knowing who we are—Partners in adventure who aren't afraid of much … any more.

We like who's at our party … and the perspective we choose to keep.

We've learned that we don't quit, and can weather almost any storm …

And to that final daunting sixth question …

… Our answer is yes, we are prepared to bet on ourselves.

We are also prepared to bet on you.

This is only the beginning.

GRATITUDE

Chapter 30

GRATITUDE ANONYMOUS

Julie and Michell

We have met so many people over the past 17 years. It has been an incredible education. People who have been mentors to us and have taught us incredible lessons, people who we have coached who have taught us incredible lessons, and mostly people who have inspired us to invest in ourselves and each other.

We are very grateful, for our lessons, our perspectives, our teachers and our opportunities. We are grateful for the chance to express our gratitude to everyone who has made a difference in our own lives.

Saying thank you is a privilege and it is a contact sport we intend to fully engage in. Having so many people to say thank you to is extraordinary evidence that wonderful people are indeed everywhere.

For your time spent reading this work, thank you.

For your refusal to back down when times get tough, thank you.

For believing in everything that's possible, thank you.

For believing in yourself, each other, and us, thank you.

We are eternally grateful.

Please visit us at **www.JulieandMichell.com** for more free tools to use.

Follow us on twitter @JulieandMichell

Until next time,

Julie & Michell

www.JulieandMichell.com

—www.thesixquestions.com—

ACKNOWLEDGMENTS

Standing in this moment is almost heart stopping.

Without the love and support of our families this dream never would have been realized.

From Julie:

To my husband, Riccardo: your unconditional support, your genius creativity, and the love you've given have guided me through the years and have elevated me to new heights. You've enlightened me with new perspectives and wisdom and helped me find inner peace. Thank you for allowing me to be me, no matter what, I'm eternally grateful. And thank you for our two beautiful boys who are the real teachers in our lives.

To my parents and my three brothers who have shaped my existence, you have been the best support system: a source so full of encouragement and guidance. Thank you Dad for your example as an author, I'm not sure how I would have started without your example and thank you mom for your courageous soul and always encouraging me to be who I want to be.

Ken Gootnick, you have been such a great mentor and healing ear for me, thank you for your wisdom and time. And thank you to all my beautiful and supportive friends; my kindred spirits, you are all blessings in my life and have filled my heart with happiness in the past, in the present, and in the future …

From Michell:

Mom and Dad, your support, encouragement and love have always been perfectly limitless. It is impossible to exaggerate the depth of the love and pride I feel to be your daughter. For everything you've done, all of our conversations, our brainstorming evenings, and all the highs and lows you've ridden right along with me my entire life—I love you and am indescribably grateful for you both.

Jesse, Dave and Heather, your encouragement and support have also meant the world. Without your technological generosity this book would still be in a pile of notebooks.

Aunt Marg Wilson, for the countless hours reading and editing, the necessary brutal candid feedback, and the resolute conviction that this would one day be published—I love you … knowing you believed in us fueled us through the rewrites.

To Leslie Tiede, thank you for teaching me to believe in myself as a businesswoman and a leader. For your generosity and incredible example as the one of the strongest women I have ever met ... thank you.

To Brendon Burchard, for more than we ever expected; *"The gift that you gave me that Sunday in September, seeing the little girl looking up at me saying 'keep going'… is a gift I will treasure for the rest of my life"... Michell*

To Alison, a world class true blue, trusted friend. The forth sister in the smith family… Your friendship is one of the most prized privileges I hold in my heart. Thank you for all that you teach me and for all of the laughter and tears… you are one in a billion.

And to everyone who has gifted me with their friendship, falling in love with people is easy when they are people like all of you…

From us both:

To Gary Polson: for your wisdom and generosity, your belief in each of us, your incredible example as a family man and as a business partner, and your continued efforts to always be so supportive throughout the years—thank you. Your guidance has been and continues to be priceless.

To Paul Gaudreau: for the incredible support you gave us both in the infancy of our careers. Thank you for believing in us and teaching us – you were the difference maker to us both.

To everyone at our incredible publisher, Morgan James Publishing—thank you a thousand times. David and Susan, Rick and Robbi, Dave and Cindy, Jim, Bethany, Margo, Morgan and Ethan, thank you for taking a chance on us and supporting us through this whole process. Working with you, the entire Morgan James team has been an honor and a privilege.

To Judith and John our editors: thank you for your investment in making sure our voices were heard throughout this work.

To Michael Ebeling for your insightful contribution in molding the final presentation of this book, thank you.

To Jere Calmes, for your generous spirit, your support, guidance, encouragement and wisdom, thank you for the tremendous assistance you have provided to us… and for the laughter.

To Jay Conrad Levinson and Jeannie Levinson: Thank you for embracing us, for teaching us, and supporting us. Working with you both has been the experience of a lifetime.

We are truly humbled by the support we have received from you all.

ABOUT THE AUTHORS

Julie Edmonds, entrepreneur, business consultant, and mother of two, founded Strictly Advertising Inc. 17 years ago after her first direct sales job after college. After receiving a BA in Finance from the University of SW Louisiana, she moved to Florida where her entrepreneurial spirit surfaced. Because of her fiercely independent and competitive nature, her business grew to generate gross revenues over one million dollars annually year after year. She has built a large organization of sales offices across the US that currently produces collectively over 8 million in direct sales annually. In 1998 she was featured in Cosmopolitan Magazine as one of 1998's Fun, Fearless, Females, showcasing her business success. Today she operates her consulting company, LNE Consulting, Inc. (*www.lneconsultinginc.com*), founded in 2009. Julie is passionate about coaching and developing young business professionals; she has helped develop and assist thousands to reach professional goals, open their own businesses and take control of their lives.

Michell Smith is a dynamic leadership and management consultant working with one of the largest direct marketing networks across North America. Located in Toronto, Canada, she founded I.C.E. Inc. in September 1996 (*www.iceinctoronto.com*) and has since built a direct sales network that at its height was comprised of over 60 managers and assistant managers, 600 sales reps and over 10 million dollars in annual revenues. Michell specializes in coaching individuals and teams to reach their highest potential by helping them define their purpose and passion. Today she continues to consult and coach hundreds of individuals, entrepreneurs, business owners, and sales reps all across North America through live seminars and private coaching sessions.

Through their careers, **Julie and Michell** have collectively coached tens of thousands of people and are well respected for their honesty and inspirational voices. They have been committed to the development of people professionally and personally and have both been consistently recognized by their peers with numerous awards for their contributions to the personal success of other entrepreneurs.

Each of them has personally conducted well over 30,000 interviews while recruiting for their sales forces, and between them, they have aided in opening over 200 companies in the past 17 years.

www.ingramcontent.com/pod-product-compliance
Lightning Source LLC
Jackson TN
JSHW081509170426
101040JS00014B/265